JUGS

I dedicate this book, with gratitude, to my mother, Hannah Clark Scott Paton, who first stimulated my interest in things artistic.

JUGS

A Collector's Guide

by
James Paton

SOUVENIR PRESS

TABLE OF CONTENTS

ACKNOWLEDGEMENTS 6

PREFACE 7

CHAPTER 1   The Earliest Jugs 9

CHAPTER 2   Stoneware – and the Ugly Mug 17

CHAPTER 3   White Stoneware 22

CHAPTER 4   Toby Fillpot 36

CHAPTER 5   Wedgwood 48

CHAPTER 6   Transfer Printing 59

CHAPTER 7   Lustre Jugs 66

CHAPTER 8   Porcelain 76

CHAPTER 9   Glass 83

CHAPTER 10   Silver 94

CHAPTER 11   Metal 102

CHAPTER 12   The American Connection 107

CHAPTER 13   Strange Shapes 112

CHAPTER 14   Commemoratives 120

CHAPTER 15   The Large and the Small 125

CHAPTER 16   The Artist Potters 129

BIBLIOGRAPHY 140

INDEX 141

ACKNOWLEDGEMENTS

So many friends who delight in the old and the curious have given help and encouragement in the formation of this book that it would be impossible to name them all here. But among those I should most like to thank are Fred Penny, Lesley Robinson, George and Grace Oakley, Joan and Fred Crickard, Helen Roberts, Pamela Wood (Nottingham Castle Museum), Lynn Daniels (Wedgwood Museum), Jennifer Metcalfe (Pilkington Museum) and Lionel A. Burman (Merseyside County Museums).

PREFACE

Little brown jug, don't I love thee . . .
That one short line from the old song sums up the whole depth of feeling that exists between men and women and their jugs.

To some it may seem strange to suggest that a sense of real affection can exist for a mere object made of china, or glass or metal. But the true collector will understand what I mean. He or she knows that highly valued possessions have a warmth, a happiness about them. Some people claim a psychic reason for this, as though an earlier owner has invested the article with his own feeling of happiness, and sometimes sadness.

Imagination? Probably. One of the greatest fascinations, which is part of collecting, is the knowledge that someone from an earlier era has shared the same pleasure of ownership. And of all the familiar articles man has manufactured to improve his life, to civilise it, the jug is for me the most important. The cup, the drinking mug, the tankard these are personal objects. But the jug is communal, something to be shared, a symbol of friendship.

Whenever a group of people first produced a vessel from which to pour water, asses' milk, or their primitive alcohol, they had taken a major step forward to becoming a community, a civilisation. When collectors of jugs pick up and handle their treasures they are aware that they hold an article that has known many convivial moments in its past – and they share that happiness all over again.

Many jugs, by their decoration, explain their own history and stimulate the imagination to step back in time. Jugs with harvest scenes will take you back to the cornfields of earlier centuries. And if you can recall hot late summer days watching the harvesters tossing sheafs of corn on to the farm wagon, before the days of the combine harvester, you will be reminded of the scents and sounds of your youth.

Jugs with hunting scenes recall the days when they may have held liquor to fill the stirrup cup of the huntsman. Toby jugs glorify the British tradition of drunkenness and conviviality; puzzle jugs the parallel tradition of enjoying a good belly laugh at the expense of someone else, preferably a stranger.

In the home the jug had its place too. Water had to be carried from the village pump, milk had to be available in the kitchen, water in the bedroom for the morning wash. Later, as life became more sophisticated, jugs were made for coffee and for claret — elegant items to add distinction to the dining room.

The history of jugs is vast and international. Europe influenced Britain with its stoneware and Delftware. Britain influenced Europe and America with its fine Staffordshire pottery from men such as Wedgwood, and its cut glass. America influenced Europe with its pressed glass .... But because the field is so vast, because there are still many thousands of old jugs still available, it is possible even today to build up a fine collection of jugs at reasonable cost.

Chapter One
THE EARLIEST JUGS

~~~~~~

The use of clay to make jugs and water-carrying vessels must be as old as man's intelligence. Clay can be found anywhere in the world. As ancient man watched pools of water forming on the ground when he looked out perhaps from the shelter of his cave, he must eventually have realised that if he could remove the impervious earth he could carry away the water with it. And then when he observed how certain kinds of earth became baked hard under the heat of the sun, he realised that he could shape the clay with his hands into shapes and sizes convenient for carrying and storing the water essential to his continued existence. The addition of a grooved lip so that the water could be poured without spilling must have been almost immediate.

Thus the first jugs must have been made at the very earliest moments of the creature that became *homo sapiens*. And as intelligence and observation evolved, so did techniques, and different materials such as metals came to be used to make vessels for water and wine.

There is evidence that early Stone Age men moulded clay into different shapes, and that the potter's wheel was in use thousands of years before the time of Christ.

Eventually potters sought ways of decorating the drab earth colours of their pottery. Jugs could be painted as they were of course, but it was not until a way was found of giving the pottery a white outer coating that really vivid effects could be achieved.

One of the earliest ways of making pottery white was used in Syria, Asia Minor and Egypt from the sixth century AD. The earthenware was covered with an opaque whitish glaze made from oxide of tin. This tin-enamelled earthenware was brought to Europe by the Moors when they occupied Spain, and it was later made in Italy and then in Holland. The ware came to be known as

Delft. It was exported from Holland to England and eventually local manufacture started, probably in London, in the middle of the 16th century.

It was also made at Bristol and Liverpool and in Ireland and Scotland.

The first English Delft jugs had a glaze splashed with blue, yellow and brown, or blue and purple. They were easily dated as they always had silver mounts, which were hallmarked.

These jugs have been given the name Malling jugs, because some have been discovered in the neighbourhood of West Malling, Kent. One dated 1581 was found in the churchyard, but as there is no evidence of there ever having been a kiln in the area it is assumed that the Malling jugs were in fact made in London.

These early jugs copied the style of stoneware jugs imported

The earliest known English jugs, made of earthenware, were tall and angular. But although many were left undecorated like this 13th century example, which is 19½ inches high, there is a pleasing boldness about their shape. *Photograph: Nottingham Castle Museum*

10

from Germany, but in the following century the English Delft potters copied the shapes of Chinese porcelain.

The most important of the potteries started in London was at Lambeth, and was in operation from the first half of the 17th century and until the end of the 18th century, producing wine bottles, fuddling cups, puzzle jugs and so on. Although decoration was varied, often the only colour used was blue from cobalt. This might be combined with ornament in white on a plain blue or greyish background, known as 'white on white' or *bianca sopra bianca*.

Before this Delft ware became fashionable in England, there had been the native style of earthenware pottery. The most usual vessels were jugs and pitchers. Those that have survived

Left: Later English earthenware jugs were boldly decorated with coloured slips. This one bears a tulip emblem and the date 1702. *Photograph: Nottingham Castle Museum*

Right: A dated lead-glazed earthenware jug, with a sgraffito cockerel and flowers, and the name Thomas Rowlands 1737. *Collection: Wally Clegg*

Delftware was being made in Liverpool in the 18th century.

This puzzle jug, dating from about 1770, has simple hand-painted decoration in blue. The verse reads:

> Gentlemen come try your skill
> I'll hold a wager if you will
> That you don't drink this liquor all
> Without you spill or let some fall.

Photograph: Merseyside County Museums

from medieval times are crude pieces of work, but there is a pleasing boldness about their shapes and styles of decoration. Jugs of the 13th century were tall and thin. In the following two centuries they became fatter and lower. Many of them were left simple and undecorated.

The English potters also found many ways of brightening up the drab clay. Much of it was covered with different coloured slips, and some vessels carried relief decoration in a clay of a different colour from that of the jug itself. They also developed a lead-based glaze which turned a yellow shade when it was fired. This yellow glaze was varied, first by adding a copper stain to produce different shades of green, and later with oxide of iron, to give rich brown shades. Glazes were applied to the jugs by daubing them on to the surface with a rag, and often only a small part of a medieval jug would be glazed.

The method of slip decoration had been known to the Romans. Slip is in fact merely clay mixed with water to make it run. It can then be applied to pottery vessels to give it an outer coat, usually of a lighter colour than the vessel itself. But it was not until the 17th century that this method of decorating pottery was fully exploited in England. After the slip was applied, by brushing or immersion, a pattern could be made either by scratching through the slip to expose the colour of the base pottery (this is known as *sgraffito*) or by tracing another colour of slip across the surface through the narrow tube of a quill.

The main centres for slip-decorated earthenware were at Wrotham in Kent, in Staffordshire and Devon, and at Harlow in Essex. Some of the jugs made at Harlow carry Puritan inscriptions in capital letters.

The Wrotham pottery dated from the start of the 17th century and carried on for about 150 years. Wrotham jugs often carry sprigged designs – that is, added relief decoration in a different coloured clay.

Many fine and elaborate harvest jugs were made in Devon, at

The happy character on this early Prattware jug appears to be counting out his pennies. Many factories produced jugs of this type in the early 19th century. *Collection: Wally Clegg*

potteries in Bideford, Remington and Barnstaple, from the beginning of the 17th century. They often carry a date and a rhyme or inscription in the *sgraffito* techniques. Some jugs have bold floral patterns, and often ships are shown in full sail. There is usually a bold chevron at the neck of Devon harvest jugs, and a coil at the bottom of the handle. The Devon potters, of whom the Fishley family was the most famous, did a thriving export business to America until Dutch Delft ware flooded the American market in the middle of the 18th century.

Another type of lead-glazed earthenware is known as Jackfield ware, although the pottery after which it is named, at Jackfield in Shropshire, was not established until around 1750, when this type of pottery had been in production for a long time. It is sometimes also called 'shining black' because it was coloured almost black by the addition of iron and manganese to the clay and glaze. Applied vine leaf decoration was then picked out in paint or gilt. Jackfield ware was also made by Thomas Whieldon and other Staffordshire potters in the late 18th century.

About this time the partnership of F. & R. Pratt of Fenton was making cheaply produced relief-moulded jugs. In quality they were inferior to the stoneware jugs being produced at the same time, but they were colourful and popular. The relief designs were picked out in colours – mainly blue and green, although yellow, purple-brown, grey-brown and black were also used. The colours had to withstand high temperatures, as they were painted or sponged on the body before firing. Afterwards the jug was given a lead glaze and refired.

The body of these early Prattware jugs (the term Prattware has come to be used recently to refer chiefly to those later products of the factory, such as pot lids, with multi-colour transfer prints) was usually white or a pale cream, and the lead glaze sometimes had a blue tinge. The quality varies a great deal. Pratt was vain enough to consider himself a better potter even than Josiah Wedgwood, but many Prattware jugs were made at other potteries, and often old worn moulds were used, giving very indistinct impressions.

The most popular designs were portraits of celebrities such as Nelson, groups of figures, grotesque caricatures of bewigged men, and hunting scenes. Probably the most famous jug is known as the Fair Toxophilite or the Female Archer. The sport of archery had become fashionable for the smart set of the early 19th century, and special archery parties were held. The Fair Toxophilite has a satirical flavour, to appeal to the humbler people who would buy such cheap jugs and delight in laughing at the antics of the idle rich.

Prattware jugs often carry the mark of such potters as Barker, Hawley, Wood and Astley.

Another type of jug, cheaply produced like Prattware and popular about the same time, is Mocha ware. Mocha jugs retained their popularity right through to the 20th century and were even copied in France.

The name comes from the Mocha stone, which in turn took its name from Mocha, the Red Sea port from which Mocha stone was

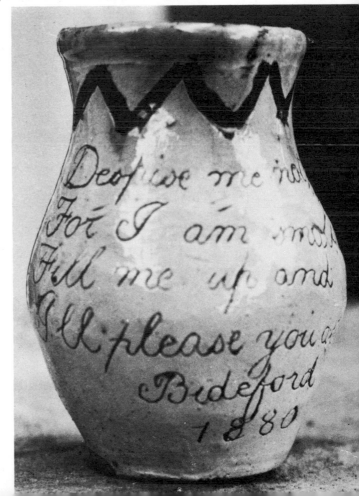

Devon has always been a centre for pottery. This jug, only 2½ inches high, bears the sgraffito inscription:
Despise me not,
For I am small.
Fill me up and
I'll please you all.
Bideford 1880.
Collection: Wally Clegg

A very good Mocha ware jug of the type used in many inns in the 19th century. It carries the standard quart measure mark. The background colour to the Mocha design is a pale blue.

exported to Europe. The stone is a type of moss agate, with fernlike striations, which the markings on the Mocha jugs resemble.

The jug would be turned upside down and a special mixture would be applied by blowpipe, or allowed to trickle across the surface of the jug while the slip coating was still wet. The potters called the mixture they used for the markings 'tea', but it was produced from tobacco juice or hops and was coloured blue, green or black by the addition of metallic oxide. Some authorities say that stale urine was used in the mixture.

The slip on Mocha jugs is applied in light-coloured bands. In early creamware Mocha jugs these bands were usually blue, yellow or brown, and in Victorian times grey and blue were common. Mocha jugs were also made in pearlware from about 1820, and in stoneware from about 1830. They were much used in taverns and in homes in the North of England.

Chapter Two
STONEWARE –
AND THE UGLY MUG

STONEWARE has very distinct advantages over ordinary earthenware. It is made from a mixture of clay and sand, which vitrifies when it is fired at a high temperature, becoming completely impermeable to liquids, even without the addition of any glaze.

It was first made in China about 1500 BC, but manufacture in Europe did not begin until about 1300 in the Rhineland. Between the 15th and the 17th centuries vast quantities of brown and grey stoneware jugs made in the Rhine Valley were exported to England.

These jugs were often called tigerware, because of their mottled markings. They ranged from six to ten inches in height and were mounted with silver or silver gilt. The top of the handle was usually about an inch below the rim of the jug, and the hinge of the domed cover raised on a box-like structure. Sometimes a band of metal round the shoulder was attached to the foot mount, with several ornamental straps secured with locking pins.

A similar type of Rhenish jug, without any precious metal mounting, proved immensely popular – the Greybeard or Bellarmine. A surprisingly large number of these jugs have survived, many hidden under the floors and hearths of Elizabethan and Stuart houses – possibly because there was a superstition that burying a drinking vessel would protect a house's occupants from evil spirits.

The neck of a Bellarmine is decorated with a grotesque bearded mask, which some people believe led to the coining of the expression 'ugly mug'.

The 'ugly mug' in question was that of the Italian Cardinal Roberto Bellarmine, and the name was given to the jug by

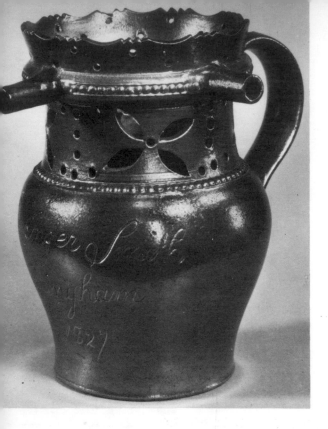

Nottingham salt-glazed stoneware. This puzzle jug is incised Inger Smith, Nottingham 1827.
Photograph: Nottingham Castle Museum

Protestant potters who ridiculed the Cardinal, saying he was 'short and stout and roundabout' – just like the jug.

Much stoneware has an orange-peel texture, caused by salt-glazing. This is done by throwing salt into the kiln at full heat. The salt reacts with the water vapour in the kiln to form a coating of silicate of soda on the pottery.

The demand for stoneware in England was so great that some enterprising man was bound to start producing it locally. That man was the famous John Dwight, once secretary to the Bishop of Chester, who founded the Fulham Pottery in 1672 after receiving a warrant from Charles II to make 'transparent earthenware or china and earthenware vulgarly called Cologne ware'. Dwight was a fine potter. He made many Bellarmine jugs, and sometimes mingled his clays so that the resultant pottery looked something like agate. Many of his jugs, silver-mounted like the imported tigerware, were of a fine grey-white salt-glazed stoneware.

He was not only an astute businessman, but also clearly something of a politician. He had received his warrant from Charles Stuart, and it might be expected when the Dutch potters John and Philip Elers arrived in England in the wake of William of Orange that Dwight would shrug his shoulders and put up with the competition. Instead, he boldly sued the Elers brothers, who had set up business in Fulham, for infringing his monopoly. But he also took care not to upset the newcomers too much, pointing out to them that London clay was not totally suitable for the type of red china they specialised in, and that much better deposits were available in Staffordshire. The Elers took his advice and set up again in Bradwell Wood, Staffordshire, where there was indeed a deposit of red clay ideal for their so-called 'fine red porcelain'.

Of course the ware made by the Elers brothers was not porcelain at all, but a very thin stoneware, in imitation of the red Yi-Hsing stoneware which was being brought in great quantities to Holland by the Dutch East India Company. The Elers' red stoneware jugs were nevertheless of a very high quality, engine-turned, and decorated with finely moulded sprigs of flowers, leaves and other motifs in relief. They also made a black stoneware, similar to the black basalt produced later by Wedgwood. Most of

The sport of bear-baiting inspired English potters to make jugs in the form of bears with dog-shaped spouts and detachable heads that could be used as drinking cups. These two splendid examples are both in salt-glazed stoneware, one from Staffordshire and the other (with chain through the bear's nose) from Nottingham. *Photograph: Nottingham Castle Museum*

their wares were unmarked, but they sometimes carry an impressed stag within a circle, and sometimes fake Chinese characters.

Other English potters started making brown stoneware around the end of the 17th century. Some of the finest jugs were produced in Nottingham, by Morleys of Mughouse Lane. These Nottingham jugs were covered with a wash of iron oxide, which gives them an iridescent brown sheen. The decoration, usually scrolls, leaves or inscriptions, was scratched on the clay surface before firing.

Tigerware was so-called because of the mottled appearance of the salt-glazed stoneware. It was exported from the Rhineland and many jugs had mounts added by London silversmiths. This jug has London hallmarks for 1576 on its silver gilt mounts. *Photograph: Nottingham Castle Museum*

One of the most curious Nottingham products was a jug in the shape of a bear, the surface being covered with clay shavings to represent the fur. The bear sits upright on its haunches and hugs a dog to its chest. The detachable head forms a drinking cup.

Similar stoneware jugs were made at Chesterfield and at Brampton in the 19th century. When a road was being built between Derby and Alfreton, the picks of the navvies revealed a stoneware clay of high quality. A potter from Belper called William Bourne bought the working rights on the land, and three years later his son Joseph founded the Denby Pottery there. Eventually at least 20 firms were producing salt-glaze stoneware in the area, and their products are now known as Chesterfield brown ware.

They made puzzle jugs and bear jugs like the Nottingham examples, but also produced many jugs with scenes in relief. There were hunting jugs, showing huntsmen and hounds chasing their quarry. And there were other jugs with simple rustic scenes – trees, windmills, beehives, men seated smoking and drinking, or in groups walking.

Some of the hunting jugs were cylindrical, more like mugs, and these were catalogued as canettes. The jugs were sold specifically for serving hot toddy or punch, as they held heat for a longer period than any comparable ware used for jugs.

These toddy jugs proved so successful that soon the London potters were producing similar jugs. John Doulton, in partnership with John Watts, was in charge of the pottery that Dwight had founded, but which now made only simple vessels such as blacking bottles and spirit jars. Under Doulton, the firm prospered, becoming the largest manufacturer of chemical stoneware in Europe, but also producing a fine series of jugs, some with scenes in relief in the Chesterfield manner; and, even more interesting and valuable for the collector of today, face jugs of famous people such as Napoleon and Nelson. Other face jugs were made at Lambeth by a firm called Bloodsworth in the High Street.

In 1835 Henry, John Doulton's second son, joined the business and soon proved himself a fine technician with an inventive mind. He was the first man to harness power to the potter's wheel, and was to lead the Doulton pottery to even greater fame. But that story I must leave to the final chapter.

Chapter Three
WHITE STONEWARE

One of the great innovators in the history of pottery was John Astbury, who was employed by the Elers brothers at Bradwell Wood. He learnt the secrets of their fine red stoneware and set up in business himself in the 1730s.

The Elers had originally described their red ware as 'red porcelain' – for they, like every other ambitious European potter of the day, were still hoping to stumble on the Chinese secret. Salt-glazed stoneware could be potted very thinly like porcelain, but it could never hope to rival porcelain because its range of colouring was so poor.

When Astbury first started in business he tried to relieve the red stoneware he produced by applying decoration in white Devon clay. But he made his greatest contribution to the potter's art when he perfected a truly white salt-glazed stoneware by adding calcined flints to a light-coloured clay mixture. He failed to produce the translucency of porcelain he had hoped for, but his new stoneware was a very fine product that could be moulded with great precision.

Astbury's new clay mixture gave potters a new versatility. Not only could it be fired and salt-glazed at a high temperature, but the same mixture fired at a lower temperature became a cream coloured earthenware. From this time there ceased to be a clear distinction between stoneware and earthenware potters.

Astbury's invention also unfortunately resulted in a new level of pollution of the air in the Potteries. So many firms started to make salt-glaze stoneware that whole neighbourhoods were thrown into smoky darkness whenever the salt was being thrown into the kilns.

Another important innovation, about 1740, was the introduction of plaster of Paris, which made it possible for multiple

Left: Relief decoration on salt-glazed stoneware jugs is usually rural and un-mistakably English, with hunt scenes and happy topers. This jug, however, bears an oriental scene, a variation of the Willow pattern that appears on so much blue and white china.

Right: Low-relief 19th century Staffordshire earthenware jug with flower decoration. *Collection: Lesley Robinson*

moulds to be produced from one master mould. So it became a much simpler matter to produce large quantities of one jug.

Astbury's own most famous jugs were a series of figure jugs in the shape of fiddlers and midshipmen. And he had working for him a young apprentice named Ralph Wood, who later made some of the first – and best – Toby jugs.

With the new techniques available, the output of jugs with relief designs increased dramatically and continued at a high level until the end of the 19th century. Among the finest white

Jean Voyez, the sculptor who offended the great Josiah Wedgwood, modelled the Fair Hebe jug, which carries his signature.

Below, left: Tam O'Shanter fleeing with witches in pursuit. The other side of this Ridgway jug shows Tam boozing with his cronies. *Collection: F. Penny*

Below, right: Interesting relief moulded jug, circa 1840, showing a happy band of monkeys guzzling wine. *Collection: Lesley Robinson*

Left: This fine relief-moulded half-gallon jug with a wide blue band at the top is typical of the work of Turners of Lane End. *Collection: Author*

Right: The colouring on this Staffordshire jug is unusual, although the foxhunt scene is common. The blue bands which form the background to the white relief design are a wishy-washy blue, like that on many Mocha ware jugs. *Collection: Author*

stoneware jugs ever produced were those made by John Turner of Lane End, particularly his jugs featuring hunting scenes in sharp relief, the rim and lip coloured blue, black or brown. Some very fine large jugs with classical reliefs and a wide dark brown collar were produced at Castleford near Leeds.

A flamboyant and now valuable jug, known as the Fair Hebe jug, bears the signature of John Voyez, who worked for various Staffordshire potters after a brief and stormy relationship with Josiah Wedgwood.

I like to think that the subject held a special fascination for the rakish Frenchman. Hebe was the Greek goddess of youth, whose chief duty was to keep the goblets of Zeus and his guests filled to the brim with nectar. She was deprived of the job by an angry

The poet Rabbie Burns appears on this relief-moulded earthenware jug. On the other side is Sir Walter Scott. Possibly made at a Scottish factory about 1840. The colour is a light blue. *Collection: Author*

White Parian jug with glazed interior, and relief classical busts in pale lilac. About 1860. *Collection: Author*

Zeus after she tripped and fell, exposing herself to the gathering in an indecent manner. Fair Hebe jugs were dated as well as signed – 1788. And because of the glaze some copies have been specifically assigned to the Ralph Wood factory, for whom Voyez worked and where he may also have assisted in the design of the first Toby jugs. Other versions of Fair Hebe from the same moulds,

This late 19th century jug was made by Copelands, and bears white Toby Fillpot relief scenes similar to those on 18th century Nottingham and Doulton stoneware. *Collection: Jean Crawford*

however, have the mark of R. M. Astbury, and later versions are painted with enamel colours instead of the Wood-type underglaze colour. The fact that this distinctive jug was probably made by several different potters is a demonstration of how difficult and dangerous it is to try to identify precisely the maker of any unmarked Staffordshire item. Workers often moved from factory to factory, and it is known that Voyez never really settled down with one employer after his early skirmish with Wedgwood. It is likely that he was allowed to take his master mould of the Fair Hebe jug with him when he left Ralph Wood.

German stoneware jug with relief frieze of dancing revellers. Probably 19th century. *Collection: F. Penny*

Charles Meigh showed his magnificent Minster jug with white relief work on a blue background at the 1851 Great Exhibition. *Collection: Author*

Many other potters made rustic jugs of unusual shapes encrusted with plant forms of every description, and sometimes resembling plant-entwined logs. Every part of the jug would be smothered in decoration, including the fancy handles and lips.

One of the most accomplished 19th-century jug makers was Charles Meigh of Hanley, who usually impressed his jugs with a description of the design and the date, as well as his own name. One buff-coloured Meigh jug shows Julius Caesar's troops landing in Britain, and on the other side Boadicea in her chariot waving her followers into battle. The inscription on the base of the jug, inside a raised relief laurel wreath, says:

Nov 1st, 1839

Published by C. Meigh

Hanley

Julius Caesar

12

Mason's are famous for their octagonal jugs, often with bright enamelling and gilding, like the jugs above. But they also produced some very fine relief-moulded jugs. The gentleman with the antlers on his head is a Celtic god call Cernuccus. The dogs on the other jug almost step out of the pottery. *Collections: Lesley Robinson and Author*

Another design registered by Meigh in 1842 was the Apostle jug. Like many other Meigh jugs, it was a Gothic shape, with a frieze of apostles standing in niches beneath arches.

W. Ridgway & Co. also produced high quality relief jugs with similar inscriptions. Their Tom O'Shanter jug, showing on one side Tam 'bousin at the nappy' with his friends, and on the other fleeing from the witches, with Cutty Sark clinging to his mare's tail, is marked underneath: Published by W. Ridgway & Co., Hanley, October 1, 1835.

These marks were much more than advertisement. They showed that the design had been registered at the Stationers' Hall in London, under the Act of June 21, 1798. This Act protected sculptural work from piracy for a period of 14 years, and made casting from any part of an original model illegal without the owner's signed and witnessed agreement.

Some Victorian potters used a so-called 'stone china' for their jugs. This new kind of pottery was first patented by the Turners

Two views of a fine Charles Meigh jug. One view shows Boadicea rallying her troops, the other shows the landing of Julius Caesar in Britain. It is dated November 1, 1839. *Collection: Author*

Early 19th-century jug with relief figures against black background. *Collection: Adrian Bowyer*

of Lane End, whose stone china was made by adding ground stone from some land belonging to the Marquis of Stafford to an earthenware clay mixture. Unfortunately the Marquis eventually ordered them to stop using the stone. If the Turners had been able to continue producing their hard stone china their pottery might not have gone bankrupt.

A patriotic stoneware jug, bearing the emblems of England, Scotland, Ireland and Wales. Like many Victorian jugs it can be easily dated from the diamond registration mark. This shows that the design was registered on October 14, 1863. *Collection: Mrs. S. Davies*

Metal lids appeared on stoneware and earthenware jugs that were used for hot water in the second half of the 19th century. This jug with a silver-plated lid dates from the 1860s. *Collection: William and Mary Leafe*

Then in 1813 another potter took out a patent for a smiliar pottery. Charles James Mason, son of porcelain-maker Miles Mason, called his strong hard earthenware Mason's Patent Ironstone China. The jugs he produced with this robust pottery are valued by collectors, and have a quite distinctive appearance. Many of the designs are oriental, with bright reds and blues and the addition of gilding. The most familiar Mason's Ironstone jugs

Simple stoneware jug with Tam O'Shanter scene. Portobello pottery, Scotland. *Collection: Author*

33

Left: An experimental coloured parian jug by Ashworth, about 1870. The pale blue colouring was streaky and unsatisfactory. *Collection: Shirley Vallance*

Right: A fine early creamware jug, possibly Leeds, with hand-painted farming and harvest scenes. 18th Century. *Collection: David Scott*

are those of eight-sided or six-sided shape, with brightly coloured Japanese patterns, and snake handles. They come in a great range of sizes, from two-and-a-half to ten inches high. But many collectors do not realise that Mason's also made buff-coloured relief-moulded jugs like the one depicting the Celtic god Cernuccus, with antlers on his head.

The Mason business prospered for a while, but eventually that firm too went bankrupt. Production of the jugs continued however because the patterns were acquired by Francis Morley, and the best known of the patterns are still in production today, with the mark Mason's Ironstone China Ltd.

Other makers of jugs with relief designs include T. R. Boote of Burslem (straight-sided jugs tapering towards the top), Cork and Edge, Holland and Green, Mintons, Copeland and J. and M. P. Bell of Glasgow.

Above, left: An unusual Ridgway jug of the 1830s with polychrome enamel birds and flowers. Dated October 1, 1835.

Above, right: This octagonal jug with Japan pattern is typical of the many Mason's Ironstone China jugs produced in great quantity and many different sizes.

Below: Staffordshire, late 18th century pottery jug with excellent hand-painted roses. The reverse has hand-painted fruit. Unmarked. *Collection: Mrs. S. Davies*

Chapter Four
TOBY FILLPOT

The English toper has been extolled in literature for centuries: from Shakespeare who created the lovable Sir Toby Belch, to G. K. Chesterton who sat in the White Hart at Beaconsfield and mused over the rolling English drunkard who made the rolling English road.

So it is not surprising that there are a number of claimants to the title of original Toby Fillpot who inspired the Toby jug.

Probably the first time the name Toby Fillpot ever appeared in print was in the song 'The Brown Jug' published in 1761:

Dear Tom, this brown jug that now foams with mild ale
(In which I will drink to sweet Nan of the Vale)
Was once Toby Fillpot, a thirsty old soul,
As e'er drank a bottle, or fathom'd a bowl;
In boosing about 'twas his praise to excel,
And among the jolly topers he bore off the bell.

It chanc'd as in dog-days he sat at his ease
In his flow'r-woven arbour as gay as you please,
With a friend and a pipe puffing sorrows away,
And with his honest old stingo was soaking his clay,
His breath-doors of life on a sudden were shut,
And he died full as big as a Dorchester butt.

His body, when long in the ground it had lain,
And time into clay had resolv'd it again,
A potter found out in its covert to smug,
And with part of fat Toby he form'd this brown jug,
Now sacred to friendship, and mirth, and mild ale,
So here's to my lovely sweet Nan of the Vale.

It is likely that by the time the Rev Francis Fawkes wrote the

Collecting Toby jugs and face jugs is not an inexpensive hobby—but it is a very satisfying one for any collector who can make a show of jugs like this. *Collection: F. Penny*

One of the most popular figures for 20th century Toby jugs has been Sir Winston Churchill. This specimen is unmarked, but Royal Doulton have also produced a fine Churchill jug. *Collection: F. Penny*

song, the name Toby Fillpot was in some sort of general usage. And two strong contenders to be regarded as the original Toby were both Yorkshiremen.

One was a notorious toper, Paul Parnell, a farmer. In the *Gentleman's Magazine* in 1810 it was stated that Parnell 'during his lifetime drank out of one silver pint cup upwards of £9000 sterling-worth of Yorkshire Stingo . . . . The calculation is taken at 2d per cupful'.

No sub-editor of today would allow such a statement to be published unchallenged. It means that Parnell must have drunk more than one million pints of beer – something like 500 pints a day every day for 60 years! Farmer Parnell must have been a mighty drinker.

The backers of the second Yorkshire challenger for the title of the true Toby Fillpot made more reasonable claims for their champion. Henry Elwes is said to have consumed 2000 gallons of strong ale from a brown jug. That would work out at about 10 pints a day for about 60 years, which is certainly beyond the capabilities of most men, but I suppose for a big-built man doing hard manual work it would not be quite impossible.

Elwes was in fact known to his cronies as Toby Fillpot. But there must have been a Toby Fillpot in every village and town towards the end of the 18th century. We must assume that the real Toby was in fact an amalgamation of many different characters right back to Shakespeare's Sir Toby Belch himself.

The credit for the invention of the first Toby jug itself is just as much shrouded in mystery, although many writers have claimed that it could have been the colourful John Voyez mentioned earlier.

Voyez, a brilliant workman, was a Frenchman who had been recruited to the potteries by Josiah Wedgwood to do sculptural work for his classical vessels. Voyez was a guest in the Wedgwood home while a house was being built for him in Burslem. But he soon upset his host. He is said to have been found working with a young and attractive nude woman posing for him, much to

Left: A beery nose distinguishes this fine early salt-glaze stoneware Toby.

Right: Another unmarked Toby — the Snuff taker — in a dark brown Rockingham glaze. This type was produced by many 19th-century potters. *Collection: Mrs. S. Davies*

A fairly conventional Toby, except for the handle, which is human form with crossed arms. 19th century. The miniature Welsh lady with shopping bag and gamp is Royal Worcester, 20th century. *Collection: Author*

Wedgwood's disgust. And both artist and model were under the influence of strong drink. The resultant row led to Voyez being sent to jail for three months.

If Wedgwood's treatment of an employee seems overbearing, and the magistrate's sentence, which also required that Voyez should be whipped with a cat o'nine tails, seems harsh, it must be remembered that these were rough and ready days in the potteries, and drunkenness was a worrying problem for factory owners. Landlords were forbidden to serve pottery workers during working hours, and in the Stoke on Trent City Museum there is a 'Tippling Notice' which was posted up in Burslem in 1815 warning publicans of this local decree.

Wedgwood continued to have a great admiration for the Frenchman's work, nevertheless, and he tried to persuade him to leave the potteries in return for a large golden handshake – so that he would not work for any of Wedgwood's competitors. Voyez refused, and went to work for Ralph Wood. Some Staffordshire jugs have been found bearing the signature of Voyez, though no Toby jug has such a mark. But even if he was not the originator of the Toby jug he almost certainly was involved in some way with the modelling of the early jugs.

Most very early jugs are in fact attributed to the factory of Ralph Wood the Elder, and his son Ralph Wood the Younger also made some fine Tobies at the Wood factory in Burslem. The Ralph Wood translucent glazes were particularly fine and have probably never been bettered in the history of ceramics. The colours were dissolved in the glaze itself, giving an impression of translucency. These early 'in-glaze' figures can be recognized by this translucent

Two more convival Tobies. The one on the left still has his hat, a bonus for the collector as these are often missing. *Collection: F. Penny*

effect, and by the fact that there were often tiny areas where the glaze, which was brushed on, had missed the biscuit surface, leaving it matt.

Towards the end of the century brighter overglaze enamels were used, including red and pink, as lower temperatures were necessary to fix the enamel colours.

Toby was such a roaring success that other factories copied him and created new versions, but as so few were marked it is difficult to state categorically that any one jug came from a particular factory.

Apart from the ordinary Toby, these are some of the other types made in the late 18th and early 19th centuries:

THE THIN MAN: A tall thin figure, holding his jug on his knee and a pipe to his mouth in the other hand. His feet rest on a raised step;

THE SQUIRE: He sits cornerwise in an armchair and holds a churchwarden pipe and a jug;

THE HEARTY GOOD FELLOW: Unusual in that he is a standing figure. He holds his hand to his heart;

THE NIGHTWATCHMAN: A white-wigged figure, carrying a lantern in one hand;

THE MAN ON A BARREL: He sits on a barrel with a jug in his hands and a dog asleep at his feet;

These Punch and Judy jugs are not so well modelled as many earlier jugs, but they still have a lot of character. The colours are ochre-red, yellow and white. *Collection: Author*

42

Something special: these First World War Tobies are now among the most coveted of all. They represent King George V and the Allied leaders, and were made at the Royal Staffordshire Pottery. The initial *F.C.G.* seen on some of the jugs are those of F. Carruthers Gould, the sculptor. This set was sold at Christies for almost £1,000 in 1974. *Photograph: Christies*

MARTHA GUNN: One of the most interesting figures, this represents a well-known Brighton bathing hut attendant of that name. A popular rhyme of Georgian days says:

> To Brighton came he
> Came George III's son,
> To be dipped in the sea
> By famed Martha Gunn.

43

Tam O'Shanter — one of the many fine face jugs produced by the Royal Doulton factory today.

The Toby jug of Martha shows her wearing an enormous plumed hat with Prince of Wales feathers and holding a gin bottle and glass.

Other early Tobies are: the Snufftaker, the Planter, the Convict, Drunken Sal, the Lawyer, the Parson, the Sailor and the Collier.

One of the charms of these early figures is that there is always some slight difference to distinguish one jug from the next, either in modelling or colouring, expression, position of the jug or pipe or other details.

After the first quarter of the 19th century Toby jugs continued to be made, but the quality deteriorated, as it did with so much of the Staffordshire pottery of the period. The modelling was not so detailed and the colours often garish.

But even if many late 19th-century and early 20th-century Toby jugs do lack some of the quality of the earliest jugs, they still have a charm of their own. Some years ago few people would have considered later Staffordshire flatback figures of little value, but the situation has changed, and these figures can now command prices in the salerooms that challenge those paid for groups by the earlier master potters. A similar situation may arise with

44

Toby jugs; in fact some of the later Toby jugs are now bringing quite big prices, especially the jugs that depict characters different from the 18th-century examples.

Two popular mid-19th-century jugs are Paul Pry and the Tythe Pig. Paul Pry was based on the meddlesome hero of John Poole's comedy of that name, published in 1825. The Tythe Pig jug shows a figure holding a pig and the curious inscription 'I will have no child tho the X pig'.

The meaning of this caption would be immediately obvious to the people of the day – and to anyone who has come across any

Made by the master. This Sailor Toby jug by Ralph Wood the Younger is inscribed 'Lord Hou' on the bottom. *Photograph: Nottingham Castle Museum*

earthenware figures or Sunderland jugs bearing this story:

In country village lives a vicar
Fond as all are of tythes and liquor
To mirth his ears are seldom shut
He'll crack a joke and laugh at smut.
But when his tythes he gathers in
True parson then, no coin no grin
On fish on flesh on birds and beast
Alike lays hold the churlish priest
Hal's wife and sow as gossips tell
Both at a time in pieces fell
The parson comes the pig he claims
And the good wife with taunts inflames
But she quite arch bow'd low and smiled
Kept back the pig held out the child
The priest look'd gruff the wife look'd big
Zounds sir quoth she, No child no pig.

Another well-made and interesting jug that appeared in the salerooms in 1975 was a five-inch-high Toby jug made by W. H. Goss, whose products have only recently been taken seriously by collectors.

A completely new pair of characters for Toby jugs were Punch and Judy, who were made in a number of different sizes, and probably in different factories. It is not easy to find a pair, and often one or both of the hats is missing. All Toby jugs originally had hats, usually designed as a drinking cup. Many of the original hats are broken, you will be lucky in fact to find a Toby jug complete with his hat.

The tradition of the Toby jug seems to be one that is likely to continue for many years in the future. One of the most collectable and valuable sets was made as late as the 1914–1918 war. This was a limited edition of jugs depicting the Allied war leaders, specially modelled by F. Carruthers Gould for the Royal Staffordshire pottery. Each of the leaders is seated, and each jug carries Gould's initials. King George V holds the world in his hands. President Wilson appears to be sitting astride a biplane. These Carruthers

Not as colourful as most Toby jugs, this one in Brampton ware, 12 inches high, is nevertheless finely modelled. Early 19th century.
Photograph: Nottingham Castle Museum

Gould Toby jugs bring high prices in London auction rooms, and a complete set is a rarity.

More familiar to the modern collector will be the Toby and character jugs made by Royal Doulton since the early 1930s. Colourful and well-modelled, these jugs have their own coterie of collectors who have started to study the marks in the hope of finding some indication that a particular jug was made in the early years of production.

At the moment Royal Doulton publish six Toby jugs: Sir Winston Churchill, Falstaff, Happy John, Honest Measure, Huntsman, and Jolly Toby. There are also seven character or face jugs, made especially to appeal to the American market, of 18th-century personalities of Williamsburg, in those days the capital of Virginia. They are the Gunsmith, the Guardsman, the Apothecary, the Blacksmith, the Gaoler, the Bootmaker and the Night-watchman. And of course there are another 45 different character jugs.

These jugs are collected today while they are still being made. As soon as one goes out of production any existing examples will start to become rarities and their value increase.

Chapter Five
WEDGWOOD

There were breweries in Staffordshire before there were potteries. So the first potteries made stoneware jugs and pots for the breweries.

The early potters earned a meagre living. Their homes were hovels. It was a time when bear-baiting, bull-fighting and drunkenness were rife. John Wesley in his journal wrote: 'March 8, 1760. Preached at Burslem, a town made up of potters. The people are poor, ignorant and often brutal . . . Several in the congregation talked out loud and laughed continuously. And then one threw at me a lump of potter's clay that struck me in the face, but it did not disturb my discourse'.

But not all the people were ignorant. The enterprising men who founded the great pottery industry also brought a new prosperity to the community, and none more successfully than Josiah Wedgwood, a self-made man who built up one of the world's most renowned potteries.

Recalling his apparently harsh treatment of John Voyez, it is enlightening to read what Wesley wrote of him: 'I met a young man by the name of J. Wedgwood, who had planted a flower garden adjacent to his pottery. He also had his men wash their hands and faces and change their clothes after working in the clay. He is small and lame, but his soul is near to God.'

At this time Wedgwood, aged 30, had only been in business as an independent potter for a year. The lameness was caused by an infection of the knee, the result of smallpox as a boy, which eventually led to his leg having to be amputated. Already his achievements were remarkable. He had been born the thirteenth child of a potter, Thomas Wedgwood, and he was a sickly boy. When he completed his apprenticeship as a potter he was penniless, but spent most of his spare time experimenting with different

Right: No, not Wedgwood, but equally good according to some collectors. This buff-coloured jasperware punch jug was made by Turners of Lane End about 1810. It carries an impressed mark, J. Mist, Fleet Street. Mist sold large quantities of Turner's pottery. *Collection: John Hamilton*

Below: The style that is synonymous with the name Wedgwood throughout the world — classical relief figures on a Wedgwood blue background. These two Jasper jugs are 19th-century examples. *Collection: F. & J. Crickard*

clays and colours. Thomas Whieldon of Fenton was so impressed by the young man's work that he took Josiah into partnership.

Whieldon's pottery was noted for its marbled and mottled glazes: his pots were dusted before firing with metallic oxides, which produced random streaky patterns in the kiln. When Wedgwood leased the Ivy House works to start on his own in

Another attractive black basalt jug. It is unmarked, and the design is not so sharp as Wedgwood's. 19th century.

1759, he produced a rich deep glaze, of a green colour. He used this glaze to imitate the cauliflowers, pineapples and cabbages which were then being made at the porcelain works in Bow and Chelsea.

Wedgwood continued to produce this cauliflower ware and marbled ware similar to Whieldon's until 1773.

But early in the 1760s he perfected his famous Queensware, with its cream-coloured earthenware body covered with a transparent lead glaze. This could be produced easily and cheaply. It was his first big success and perhaps his greatest; and it has remained the chief manufacture of Wedgwoods for 200 years. The earthenware was called Queensware after Queen Charlotte, who appointed Wedgwood Potter to the Queen. Similar creamware was soon being made by many other potters, notably at Leeds.

Wedgwood's financial success seemed assured. But that was not enough for him. Apart from the fact that he had a restlessly inquiring mind, his greatest dream, perhaps the spur for all his ambition, had not been achieved.

When he was 19 Wedgwood, the penniless apprentice without prospects, had fallen in love with Sarah Wedgwood, daughter of his father's cousin, a retired cheesemonger from Cheshire. Sarah did not rebuff the sickly young man, and her father was tolerant. But it was made absolutely clear to Josiah that he could not hope to marry a young woman of her standing, who would one day be heiress to £10,000. Any suitor must be able to show equal prospects.

Josiah was forbidden to make the journey of 40 miles to Sarah's

home, but after a year this requirement was relaxed and an understanding developed that when Wedgwood had £10,000 to his name, the marriage could take place. No doubt the old cheesemonger thought such a sum would always be beyond Josiah's grasp. So when Josiah proved to him that his now successful business was worth the magic sum, the old man replied that Sarah's dowry had increased through wise investments. Eventually, however, as the old man saw how Josiah prospered, he relented, and the couple were married at Astbury in Cheshire in 1764.

Moonlight lustre jug. Early 19th century. *Wedgwood Museum Trust*

Sarah's inheritance of £20,000 helped Wedgwood to build his famous works which he called Etruria. The demand for his creamware was now so huge that the Staffordshire factory's decorators could not cope with the work, so much of the creamware was sent to Liverpool to be decorated with transfer prints by the firm of Sadler and Green, inventors of the process.

After about 15 years some of Wedgwood's aristocratic customers complained that they were getting tired of the yellowish colour. Wedgwood met their objections by making an almost white ware which he called pearlware. Different glazing techniques were also used on creamware to imitate the marbles of the classical vases, ewers and urns at the time being brought back to England

52

by ladies and gentlemen who had been on the Grand Tour. Granite, pebble and marble glazes were developed, and Wedgwood also introduced an agate body, in which the marbled effect went right through the pottery. This was done by kneading together different coloured clays.

The next significant invention by Wedgwood was black basalt, a dense blackware which did not need glazing. He used this to imitate Etruscan ewers and vases. The Greek technique had been to make the ewers in red clay, coated with a black slip, except where the red figures showed through. But Wedgwood's ewers have a black body, with the red figures painted on top. Black basalt was also used for relief moulding, which was always classical.

The Etruscan ware was extremely popular for a while. In one year the factory had orders for 350 classical ewers and 145 vases in one design alone. Early Wedgwood black basalt jugs and ewers are now scarce.

Drabware, circa 1830. The name is self-explanatory. *Wedgwood Museum Trust*

But the best known of all Wedgwood productions is jasper ware. This distinctive pottery, usually featuring white relief figures on a Wedgwood blue background, was first produced in 1775, after many experiments over a long period. It was not always blue, however; it was also made in green, black, lilac, grey and a pinkish colour. It was difficult to colour and fire, so for once Wedgwood had little trouble with imitators. Probably only the Turner and Adams firms had any competitive success in the making of jasper ware.

Sometimes the blue colour of the jasper would bleed into the white relief figures, particularly with the darker blue pieces. To avoid this, considerable use was made of jasper dip – instead of being coloured right through, the clay was dipped into a slip to give it a coating of colour.

Although jasper is the best known of all Wedgwood's pottery,

A collection of Wedgwood table pottery in black basalt and marbled ware. The little marbled cream jug with a side handle in the bottom left-hand corner is a rare and unusual item. Whieldon-Wedgwood type ware about 1755–58. *Wedgwood Museum Trust*

he also made other unglazed stonewares coloured right through the clay. Rosso Antico, for example, was the superior name Wedgwood gave to his version of Staffordshire red stoneware. And Caneware, coloured a soft buff yellow, was shaped into groups of imitation bamboo canes for jugs and teapots with imitation bamboo handles.

After the first Josiah Wedgwood died in 1795, a wealthy man, the firm's prosperity declined. The Napoleonic wars were a difficult period for all business, and Josiah II, understandably, lacked the drive and ability of his father. The firm became copyists instead of innovators. In 1812 the Wedgwood factory began to

19th-century bone china. Hand-painted scenes of English landscapes, with gold line decoration. *Wedgwood Museum Trust*

Caneware, circa 1810. *Wedgwood Museum Trust*

Smear-glaze Gothic-style pitcher 1840–50. *Wedgwood Museum Trust*

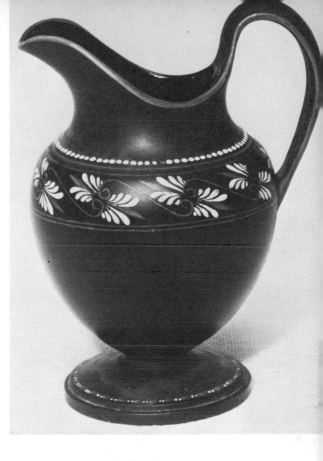

Black basalt jug, encaustic-painted decoration. Marked Wedgwood and Bentley, 1770s. *Wedgwood Museum Trust*

produce bone china, which had been introduced by Josiah Spode at the end of the 18th century. For the first time Wedgwood jugs were decorated with Chinese motifs imitating porcelain designs – with prancing dragons and bold flowers. Oriental decoration was also put on to a matt terracotta or black body. Departing from Wedgwood tradition, there was no relief ornamentation, but shiny flowers and other motifs were painted on to the matt body.

It is interesting that very little underglaze blue transfer-printed ware was ever made by Wedgwood. The firm continued with the earlier overglaze black transfer printing long after other potteries had turned to using the blue. No Wedgwood design in underglaze blue can be earlier than 1806. In fact the firm was content to produce utilitarian wares until the 1870s, when old Wedgwood began to be collected eagerly. Old designs

were reissued by the factory, sometimes in new colours, and from 1878 bone china was made again. This revival formed the base for the great 20th-century expansion of the firm, and some of the Wedgwood of this century is now sought by collectors.

Daisy Mackeig-Jones adapted early experiments with a dappled glazing known as moonlight lustre, and other richly coloured glazes for designs in chinoiserie and art nouveau. Two names are used for her pieces – Fairyland Lustre and Dragon Lustre. A printed outline was painted in by hand, before the piece was glazed. The lustre was then applied and fired, and the original outline was overprinted in gold. These designs were continued until 1939.

Another Wedgwood designer who did fine work during the 1930s was Keith Murray, whose inspiration came from Chinese wares and Korean pottery, making good use of engine-turned decoration. His pieces have a semi-matt glaze, usually in off-white or grey-green.

58

Chapter Six
TRANSFER PRINTING

The Liverpool contribution to the development of the British pottery industry is not always fully appreciated. There is little doubt that jugs and mugs made from the local red clay were being produced in Liverpool in the 17th century, when the city was a relatively small town of less than 30,000 inhabitants.

In the early years of the following century a number of potters moved from Southwark to Liverpool, where they began to produce tin-glazed earthenware. Alan Smith records in his booklet *Liverpool Pottery* that the first reference to Delftware in Liverpool was made on April 23 1712, when Nicholas Blundell wrote in his diary: 'I went with Molly to ye whit-mettle house (white metal meaning tin-glaze) and bought a punch bowl.' On another occasion Blundell refers to buying an ornamental jug, which he broke before he got home with it. By the middle of the 18th century there were more than 20 factories making earthenware and porcelain, and it was about this time that John Sadler and Guy Green were working on experiments that were to revolutionise the decoration of pottery, and to make possible the mass production of decorated wares.

They were well aware of the importance of their first transfer prints on delft tiles, for they swore in an affidavit in the presence of a lawyer in 1756 that they 'without the aid or assistance of any other person or persons did, within the space of six hours ... print upwards of twelve hundred earthenware tiles of different patterns, at Liverpoole aforesaid, and which ... were more in number and better, and neater than one hundred skilful pot painters could have painted in the like space of time'.

The process used by Sadler and Green was to take a print on a thin piece of tissue paper from a wood block, transferring the print on to glazed pottery, then firing the piece again at a low

A Staffordshire blue and white jug, with transfer-printed hunting scene.

temperature to fuse the colour into the glaze.

Soon Sadler and Green found that an engraved copper plate gave a clearer picture than wood blocks, and that they could also transfer prints to the curved surfaces of jugs and other hollow wares.

The new decoration was ideal for the soft paste porcelain made in Liverpool, but even more so for the new creamware invented by Josiah Wedgwood at Stoke on Trent. In fact, the new development could not have come at a better time for Wedgwood, who would not otherwise have been able to decorate all the creamware ordered from him. Wedgwood insisted on improvements in the Liverpool designs. He wrote scornfully of Sadler's 'childish scrawling sprigs of flowers for the rims, all of which he thinks very clever, but they will not do for us'. Sensibly, Sadler adapted his designs to suit Wedgwood, and the arrangement whereby Sadler and Green decorated Wedgwood creamware with their black overglaze transfer prints lasted for some time, until Wedgwood, like other Staffordshire potters, set up his own transfer printing section. Wedgwood in fact, continued with black overglaze printing for a much longer period than did most other

60

potters, who found that the designs too easily became worn and rubbed.

Some of the Wedgwood wares printed by Sadler were sold independently by the Liverpool man, some were returned to Wedgwood for his own customers, and some were exported direct from Liverpool to America.

This business arrangement led to Wedgwood making frequent visits to Liverpool, where he met his great friend and eventual partner, the Liverpool merchant Thomas Bentley.

Wedgwood's enterprise also spelt the beginning of the end for the Liverpool potteries. He instigated the building of the Trent and Mersey Canal in 1766, which eventually provided a cheap and easy mode of transport for Staffordshire pottery to the Liverpool docks. Without the natural resources of abundant clay such as existed in Staffordshire, the Liverpool firms gradually went out of business (with one notable exception).

Before that happened, however, the Liverpool factories, like all the Staffordshire ones, copied Wedgwood's new creamware. Jugs made of Liverpool creamware are heavier and thicker-bodied than the best products of Leeds and Staffordshire, but their makers did bring an elegant and distinctive new shape into being, which has become known simply as the Liverpool jug. Many of these jugs were exported to America, and the shape was in fact

A magnificent example of black overglaze transfer printing, in which the Liverpool factories excelled. This 12-inch high earthenware jug made at the Herculaneum factory about 1837 has transfer prints inside the jug as well as outside. The view of George's Parade Liverpool is believed to have been adapted from an engraving published in The Lancashire Illustrated in 1832. *Photograph: Merseyside County Museums*

Bridges and boats often appear on old blue and white underglaze transfer print jugs like this one.

copied by the American silversmith Paul Revere.

Most Liverpool creamware jugs were unmarked, until the most famous Liverpool factory of all came into being – the Herculaneum Pottery.

This grandiose name was chosen by the Liverpool merchants who combined to start the factory to rival Wedgwood's Etruria. Some very fine work, notably transfer-printed jugs, was produced by Herculaneum before it eventually succumbed to Staffordshire

The rural 'Harvest Home' scene on this Herculaneum jug is an overglaze transfer print in puce. It is 7 inches high and is signed 'Johnson, Liverpool'. Date about 1800. *Photograph: Merseyside County Museums*

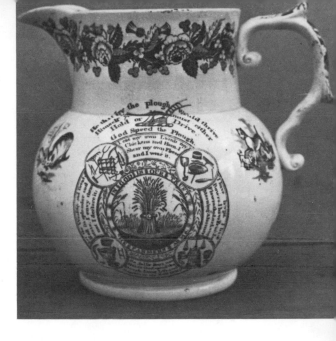

Farmer's Arms jug with overglaze black transfer prints. Probably Sunderland, early 19th century.
Collection: Adrian Bowyer

competition in 1840. One reason why Herculaneum survived so much longer than the earlier Liverpool firms was the fact that it was built on the banks of the Mersey, with its own docks. Three-quarters of its production was exported, not only to the United States but also to Canada, Brazil, Peru, Chile, the East Indies and Africa. Many Herculaneum designs were made specifically for the American market, and collections in the United States contain many examples not found in Britain.

Although Liverpool potters, like Wedgwood, did eventually use underglaze transfer printing in blue, they also continued to use the overglaze black transfer prints invented by Sadler and Green. The advantage of the underglaze printing was that the designs were not so easily damaged. Cobalt-based blue was used because it could withstand the high kiln temperatures. The disadvantage was that the underglaze prints did not have the same precise definition as the overglaze black printing. No underglaze blue transfer print could ever, for instance, have the same quality as the earthenware Herculaneum jug with engravings both inside and out which I have illustrated. The fine scene of George's Parade, Liverpool, was adapted from an engraving in *The Lancashire Illustrated* in 1832.

63

Although Sadler and Green are accepted as the originators of transfer printing, the process was used independently in other places. It was used for enamel wares at Battersea, and was adapted for use on porcelain by Robert Hancock in 1756 at Bow and Worcester, in the same year that Sadler and Green swore their affidavit. Perhaps they had heard of this work elsewhere, and as they had already been experimenting with transfer printing for seven years, wanted to ensure that no one would steal their glory.

In addition to black overglaze printing, some Liverpool potters used red and lilac.

The process of underglaze blue printing was introduced by Hancock at Worcester in 1759, and its use spread to other porcelain factories before Josiah Spode introduced it to Staffordshire about 1781. The clarity of the blue transfer printing improved after 1806, when better quality transfer paper was introduced.

Eventually the problem of underglaze printing in other colours than blue was solved, and pink, brown and green were used from 1828, although the blue always retained its popularity. Three colours were used on a single transfer paper from the 1840s.

No problem about dating this jug. The original owner saw to that. It carries 'God Speed the Plough' transfer prints in black. *Collection: Adrian Bowyer*

The stoneware jug on the left depicts the same drinking scene as the one on the black transfer-printed tile in the centre. The one on the right is glazed internally and cast in buff and cream from marbled liquid clayslip. Classical reliefs applied in white. Herculaneum factory 1805–10. Height 6¾ inches. *Photograph: Merseyside County Museums*

The fact that transfer printing threatened their future naturally made artists rebellious. To meet the complaints of men threatened with redundancy, Spode and other potters introduced the practice of overglaze hand colouring on underglaze printed outlines. The colour was washed in carefully with enamels, and one transfer print could be used to produce many differently coloured versions of the same design.

At Worcester, this technique was also used for some of the early mandarin patterns in the Chinese style on porcelain.

But the apex of Victorian transfer printing was reached when F. and R. Pratt of Fenton adapted the methods used for multi-colour printing by George Baxter in his famous series of prints published between 1828 and 1860. Each tint required a different engraving, so that a large number of transfers had to be used for each picture. The most famous of their products were of course pot lids for pomade and fish paste, but jugs and other table ware were also produced. Pratt's chief engraver and designer was Jesse Austin, whose signature or initials can often be seen on the prints he personally engraved.

Chapter Seven
LUSTRE JUGS

To many collectors the word 'lustre' is almost synonymous with Sunderland, where much of the most interesting English pottery originated in the 18th and 19th centuries. But the practice of coating pottery with an iridescent lustre is a very ancient one.

The first lustre pottery was probably produced in the Islamic world about the year 850 AD. Egyptian lustre pottery has been dated to about 1100, and the manufacture of fine lustre ware continued in Persia from the 12th to the 17th century. In Europe lustre pottery was produced in Spain and Italy during the Middle Ages. But the techniques used in this early lustre pottery did not appeal to the British. They were costly, and losses in firing were extraordinarily high. The prospect that about three-quarters of your production would be useless when it came from the kiln was not economically encouraging.

Two factors tempted the Staffordshire and Sunderland potters eventually to produce lustre pottery. One was the success of Sheffield plate in capturing a large slice of the market for silver-ware. If the Sheffield business men could make a killing by coating copper with a thin film of silver, and thus undercutting the prices of the silversmith, could not the clever potter coat earthenware with a similar film of silver, and undercut even the prices of the Sheffield experimenters? The second factor – which made these ambitious ideas realistic – was the discovery of platinum in 1750. The new metal was found to be even more lustrous than silver, and to be unaffected by the atmosphere, and even by acid and alkali.

Attempts to coat ordinary red or brown clay with silver-based lustre had proved to be disappointing: the resultant wares lacked brilliance. But John Wilcock of Hanley successfully produced a platinum-based silver lustre about the end of the 18th century.

The new 'silver' jugs, teapots and other vessels never really competed with the genuine article. But humble people were able to afford flashy-looking pottery, and the potters themselves went on to make more use of the other kinds of lustre – gold or copper lustre (the actual base material was in fact gold in the English process), 'resist' and stencilled lustre, and pink lustre.

The phrase 'resist' lustre describes those articles in which the lustre forms a background to the main design. But it is the pink lustre, used so much in Sunderland ware, that is of main interest to the collector of jugs. Pink lustre is gold lustre which has been applied over pottery with a white body or a white glaze: the gold solution appears on this white background in all shades from pale pink to deep purple, depending on the thickness of the solution. The term 'Sunderland lustre' is nowadays used to describe a speckled pink variety. But exactly the same effect was produced at potteries in Staffordshire, Bristol and Liverpool. Sunderland became so closely linked with this type of pottery partly because of the large output of the potteries in that area, and the export of their jugs, vases, bowls, frog mugs and other wares to Europe and America. But a more important reason is probably the fact that so many of the transfer-printed designs used on this type of jug were recognisably from that area. What more recognisable design

Left: This 19th-century Staffordshire mask lip jug has the unusual combination of copper lustre for the upper half and a marbled pottery for the lower half. *Collection: Mrs. S. Davies*

Right: An unusual silver resist lustre jug. It also has white relief floral decoration around the rim. About 1830. *Collection: Mrs. S. Davies*

Left: Pink mottled lustre with slave-trade verse. Garrison pottery.

Below: 'Cottage' ware jugs and plate decorated with speckled pink lustre. Possibly made at the Garrison pottery. *Photographs: Sunderland Museum*

is there than the Sunderland Bridge? Surely no monument in all history has been so celebrated by the potter's craft.

The true name of the bridge was the Wearmouth Bridge, the longest single-span cast-iron bridge in the world at the time

Copper lustre jug with relief farming scenes in bright polychrome colours. Although the handle is broken, some early collector has replaced it with a pewter handle and lid. Circa 1820. *Collection: Adrian Bowyer*

it was opened in 1796. The span was 236 feet, the height from low-water mark 100 feet and the spring of the arch 33 feet – all facts faithfully and admiringly recorded by the potters of Wearside on many thousands of jugs.

In 1858 Robert Stephenson the engineer advised that there were serious faults in the bridge, and it was reconstructed. The widened and strengthened bridge remained in use until the nineteen twenties, when it became overloaded with motor traffic, and a new bridge was opened in 1929 by the Duke of York, later George VI.

In the Sunderland Museum there are 33 different transfer-printed views of the Wearmouth Bridge as it appeared on pottery. Most were in black, but some were in blue and green, and many were hand coloured. Every one of these 33 views is illustrated in a booklet *Sunderland Ware* published by the museum. A commemorative jug was produced after the rebuilding in 1929 by the

Wearside Pottery Company, Millfield, with the new bridge illustrated in relief.

A large number of potteries produced the Sunderland jugs, making use of the plentiful brown clay in the area. It was also cheap to import white clay, as colliers returning to Sunderland were happy to accept cargoes at a low price.

Above, left: Jug of unusual shape, with transfer print of the ship Agamemnon in a storm.

Above, right: Jug decorated with pink lustre bands and splashes. Transfer printed verse on one side and Wearmouth Bridge on the other. About 1820.

Left: Punch jug and cover. Very early 19th century. The rural scene is a black overglaze transfer print. *Photographs: Sunderland Museum*

The first of these potteries was founded at Newbottle, a village a few miles outside Sunderland, in about 1720. And a century later 300,000 pieces were being exported annually from the various potteries in the area.

Many of the scenes and rhymes to be seen on Sunderland jugs reflected the seafaring and farming traditions of the North-East of England. Great naval feats such as the Battles of the Nile and Trafalgar were recorded in verse.

Perhaps the best of the farming inscriptions is this one seen on a number of jugs:

Let the wealthy and great
Roll in splendour and state,
I envy them not I declare it,
I eat my own lamb,
My chicken and ham,
I shear my own fleece and I wear it.
I have fruits I have flowers,
I have lawns I have bowers,
The lark is my morning alarmer.
So jolly boys now
Here's God speed the plough,
Long life and success to the farmer.

Right: God Speed the Plough jug, with farming transfer print.

Left: An east view of the Wearmouth Bridge. *Photographs: Sunderland Museum*

This dated bridge jug carries the inscription on one
side 'Goevan Mowbray 1836', and this verse:
'Tell me ye knowing and discerning few
Where I may find a friend both just and true
Who dare stand by me when in deep distress
And then his love and friendship do most express'
Photograph: Sunderland Museum

Then a Freemason's jug from the Garrison Pottery proclaims:

Let masonry expand from pole to pole
After sacred laws expand,
Far as the mighty waters roll.
To wash the remotest land.
That virtue has not left mankind
Her social maxims prove,
For stamped upon the mason's mind
Are unity and love.

There is occasionally cautious advice:

Come my old friend and take a pot
But mark now what I say –
While that thou drink'st thy neighbour's health
Drink not thine own away.
It but too often is the case while we sit o'er a pot,
We kindly wish our friends good health
Our own is quite forgot.

72

Above, left: Jug with 2½-gallon capacity, with extra holding handle below spout. Decorated with pink lustre bands and transfer-printed design of three ships. West view of the Wearmouth Bridge. About 1813–20. *Photograph: Sunderland Museum*

Above, right: Silver resist jug with masonic emblems. Staffordshire about 1830. *Collection: Adrian Bowyer*

Below, left: It was common in the 19th century for innkeepers to have the pub's name printed on jugs, to discourage pilferers. This jug has a wide copper lustre band at the top. *Collection: Mrs S. Davies*

A simple copper lustre jug. 19th century. *Collection: Adrian Bowyer*

Courtship and marriage is of course a frequent subject:

My lad is far upon the sea,
His absence makes me mourn,
The bark that bears him far from me
I hope will safe return.

And from his earning I'll save up
If lucky he should be,
And then when old with me shall stop
And go no more to sea.

But could the girl patiently waiting at home be sure of her sailor boy's fidelity?

What should sailors do on shore
But kiss the girls and toss the can;
When the cannons cease to roar
Sweet's the voice of smiling Nan.

The jugs and other pottery bearing these and similar descriptions were often made for presentation purposes – to mark baptisms, birthdays, weddings, as well as famous events. One of the most popular designs records the bravery of a local hero,

Jack Crawford, who climbed his ship's mast at the Battle of Camperdown in 1797 to nail up the Union Jack. The verse on one jug goes:

> At Camperdown we fought
> And when at the worst of the fray
> Our mizzen near the top, boys,
> Was fairly shot away
> The foe though we had struck,
> But Jack cried out 'Avast',
> And the colours of Old England
> He nailed up to the mast.

The size of some of these Sunderland jugs is often remarkable, some being big enough to hold two and a half gallons of water. Of course there was no piped water supply in those days, and large jugs were used to carry water into the home. These jugs were also often produced in sets of up to a dozen, ranging down from the two-and-a-half-gallon giant size to a tiny cream jug.

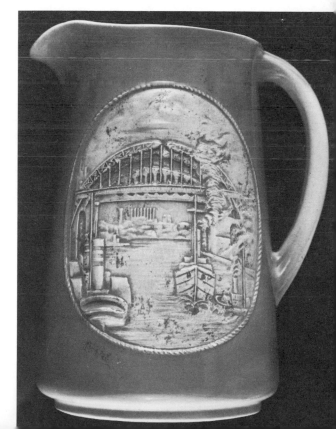

Earthenware jug. Relief view of Wearmouth Bridge after it was rebuilt in 1929. Wearside Pottery Co., Millfield. *Photograph: Sunderland Museum*

Chapter Eight
PORCELAIN

For more than 200 years Europeans were mystified by the translucent pottery from China they called porcelain. They were envious too of the way this porcelain began to dominate the luxury market.

But it was not until 1709 that Johann Bottger discovered that the secret lay in the use of kaolin in the mixture. It was fortunate for Bottger that he succeeded in this enterprise, for he had earlier been jailed by Augustus the Strong of Saxony for failing to keep a promise to turn lead into gold. But as it turned out his discovery of the secret of ancient Cathay was almost as profitable as he had hoped alchemy would be. The porcelain factory set up at Meissen by Augustus became the most renowned of all time.

The secret was well guarded for years, although workers who deserted Meissen eventually took it with them, first to Vienna and then to Venice. But in the meantime the ambitious French and English potters who sought to make porcelain had to make do with artificial mixtures which came to be known as soft-paste, as against the hard paste of the real porcelain.

These soft-paste porcelains had a charm of their own, and when the secret of kaolin became universally known, most of the English potters didn't use it: they preferred the methods they had developed themselves.

Some splendid jugs were made at Meissen, and also at the French factories, such as St Cloud, Sèvres and Vincennes. And the earliest known piece of English soft-paste porcelain was also a very fine jug, modelled by Nicholas Sprimont, a Huguenot silversmith. An example of this famous 'goat and bee' jug can only now be afforded by a very wealthy collector.

The 'goat and bee' jug was a cream jug, the lower part of whose body was shaped in the form of two reclining goats. There was usually a bee in applied relief below the lip, and the handle was a branch. Some are marked 'Chelsea 1745' with an incised triangle, and others just have the triangle. The same design was used about the same period for silver jugs, and at a later date forgeries were made in cast silver, taken from the porcelain jugs.

Sprimont, the originator of this Chelsea jug, had been appointed manager of the Chelsea works, many of whose jugs and other designs were also adaptations of silver originals. But this was also true of all the earliest porcelain, and Nicholas Sprimont,

Chinese porcelain. A famille verte helmet jug, 10 inches high. K'ang Hsi period (1662–1722). *Photograph: Phillips*

Left: The Chelsea 'Goat and Bee' jug. This was the earliest piece of porcelain known to have been made at an English factory.

Right: 18th-century Worcester 'Cabbage Leaf' jug, with mask lip. *Collection: Mrs. S. Davies*

a flamboyant character who drove around London in a gilded coach, was a good choice to run the first English porcelain factory.

At Ludwigsburg in Germany they actually made jugs standing on three legs – appropriate enough for silver, but somehow not right for porcelain.

In general cream jugs and the like produced by British factories tended also to follow this imitative fashion, so the shapes often continued to be modelled as silver jugs. Sparrow-beaked jugs, copied from silver shapes, were made at Bow, Worcester and Lowestoft. These were pear-shaped with a loop or simple scrolled handle. The body was normally plain, but sometimes it was fluted.

For the wealthy collector only — this early Meissen milk jug and cover, 7 inches high, is decorated with Chinese figures tooled in gold by Bartholomaus Seuter of Augsburg. It has silver gilt mounts. *Photograph: Phillips*

Two New Hall cream jugs.

The face on the mask lip of this jug, one of the most desirable pieces of Derby porcelain, is that of Lord Rodney, the naval hero. *Courtesy Sothebys*

There were, however, some distinctive British designs in porcelain. One of the great successes of the Derby factory, which took over the Chelsea mantle when that firm closed, was the Lord Rodney jug, made to commemorate that admiral's victory over the French in the West Indies in 1782. The spout was moulded in the shape of the admiral's face, a little like the figurehead of one of his ships.

At Worcester, in the early Dr Wall period (1751–1783), a strange new jug was designed and successfully marketed. It was known as the cabbage leaf jug, because it was moulded in the form of overlapping cabbage leaves, and had no lip. Later examples were supplied with a mask lip.

All Worcester of this period is beautifully decorated in striking colours. Birds, butterflies and flowers were printed on white panels set against a coloured background, perhaps pink, yellow, blue or apple green. The artists responsible were mostly men who had worked at Chelsea and moved to Worcester in the 1760s.

Knowledgeable collectors of Worcester look out for special rarities, such as early jugs and mugs in blue and white which are marked with a cross cut into the paste.

Some jugs and vases from Worcester bore the famous Long Eliza figures – slender tall ladies copied from Chinese designs. This Long Eliza design was also used later on Liverpool porcelain, but the quality of the Liverpool enamelling was cruder.

Caughley in Shropshire also used the Long Eliza pattern. This factory copied the cabbage leaf jug with mask lip – some examples are decorated with printed views of the bridge over the Severn at Ironbridge.

The only true hard-paste porcelain in Britain was developed at Plymouth, and was later carried on at Bristol and New Hall. William Cookworthy, a Plymouth chemist, discovered the magic ingredient kaolin in Cornwall and took out a patent for what he described as 'New Invented Porcelain' and set up in business in 1768. His factory was not a success, and after only two years the business was transferred to Bristol. The patent rights were

Left: The simplistic but bold and attractive floral decoration on this early Liverpool porcelain jug is in underglaze blue. Dated about 1760, it came from Richard Chaffer's factory. *Photograph: Merseyside County Museums*

Right: Satsuma jug. This type of porcelain was produced in the Satsuma Province of Japan in the 18th and 19th centuries. It is heavily gilded and enamelled to give a brocaded effect.

New Hall sparrow beak cream jug.

bought from Cookworthy by Richard Champion. But he was no more successful, and eventually sold his rights to a group of Staffordshire potters who set up the New Hall factory at Shelton in 1781. The most attractive of the Bristol and New Hall porcelains were the more modest wares, known as 'cottage china'. The decoration is simple, sprigs, roses and ribbons, and it is ungilded. Pinks, reds and greens are the favourite colours.

Although porcelain tableware was often made in sets, it is now quite common, and not prohibitively expensive, to collect just the cream jugs either of the factory of your choice, or of various British porcelains-makers. As fashions changed, so did the shape of the cream jugs, so such a collection can provide considerable variety.

A beautiful hand-painted Worcester jug, 8 inches high, first period.
Photograph: Nottingham Castle Museum

Chapter Nine
GLASS

The story of how glass was discovered is lost in antiquity. It is known that the Egyptians made glass between 4000 and 5000 years ago, but no one has come up with a better story of how it all started than that told by Pliny.

Merchants sailing in the Mediterranean went ashore one night to camp by a river estuary, he claims. They used blocks of natron (a type of soda) to support their cooking pots above the fire they made. Later they found that heat had fused the natron and sand together, forming a completely new and strange substance – glass.

No doubt Pliny's story was not far from the truth, although when he wrote glass had been manufactured for around 3000 years. It seems natural that glass-making should have developed from men observing and copying some accidental occurrence.

The Egyptians and the Syrians were the earliest glass-makers, followed by the Romans, who knew everything about glass except how to make crystal glass. They engraved, enamelled and gilded glass, and made it in a variety of colours. Naturally the art of glass-making spread throughout the Roman Empire. And when the Empire shrank in the Dark Ages, the Seine and Rhine became the chief glass-making areas. The Angles and Saxons who invaded Britain brought their glass vessels with them, and many jugs of the type made on the Rhine and Seine in the second and third centuries have been found at Colchester and other places.

All these early jugs are now museum pieces, however, beyond the means of the ordinary collector, as is much of the glass of the Middle Ages, made in Venice, Bohemia, the Netherlands and France.

In England there was some glass-making in the Weald area of Surrey, and in the 16th century continental glassmakers, notably Verzelini, brought the making of glass in the delicate, highly

Right: A rare Ravenscroft jug, made around 1680–90, used for honey syllabub, a popular drink. *Photograph: Phillips*

Left: Decanter jug, English, c. 1685. With stopper, 5⅛ inches high.

Below: Three fine Georgian engraved jugs. The centre one carries the date 1797. *Photograph: Phillips*

Jug excavated at Karak, Jordan. Mould blown in amber glass, $5\frac{1}{2}$ inches high, base $2\frac{1}{2}$ inches with pearly blue iridescence. 578–636 AD.
Photograph: Pilkington Museum

decorated Venetian style to London.

Venetian glass, however, was fragile, and too thin for engraving. A wealthy British shipowner called George Ravenscroft, who had an interest in and knowledge of chemistry, was convinced he could improve the quality of glass. He began experiments that were to revolutionise glass-making and to make England the most important centre of the trade. The influential Company of Glass Sellers recognised his potential – as they had with pottery-maker John Dwight at Fulham – and backed him financially. At first he worked at a glasshouse in the Savoy, but later set up a new establishment at Henley on Thames, far enough away from London to thwart the activities of industrial spies.

Ravenscroft's early attempts at producing clear crystal glass suffered from 'crizzling' which clouded the glass, but eventually after many experiments he cured the fault by adding lead oxide.

Right: Four-sided moulded jar, Syrian, 1st–2nd century AD. $10\frac{1}{4}$ inches high in sea-green glass.

Left: A jug from The Roman Empire, possibly Egypt. First half of 4th century AD. $8\frac{1}{4}$ inches high in pale green glass. Attached to the rim which is folded back on itself and ridged, is a wide plain handle set on the 12-sided spirally ribbed body. *Photographs: Pilkington Museum*

It is possible that the idea of using lead may have occurred to him because so much English earthenware was glazed with lead.

Ravenscroft's new glass, strong and clear, and thick enough for elaborate engraving, made England the leader in the world's glass markets.

It is the period from Ravenscroft onwards that is of greatest interest for the glass collector. One would have to be wealthy indeed to be able to afford a unique and beautiful jug like the Ravenscroft syllabub jug illustrated – it brought £2,500 at Phillips auction rooms in London in 1974 – but there are beautiful Georgian glass jugs in old English lead glass within the reach of many collectors.

The syllabub jug has the words 'Honey Syllabub' gilded below the neck. Syllabub, according to a recipe in *The Compleat House-wife* (1732), was prepared from cream and sack, with some lemon juice, and whipped to a froth. As a guide to value, the three fine 18th-century engraved jugs were also sold at Phillips in 1974 for £110, £95 and £120.

The chief form of decoration on glass jugs of the 18th century is wheel engraving – which involves grinding out the design with small copper wheels in a lathe. The best engravers were Dutch,

Left: Jug, Roman, 1st–2nd century AD. 10¼ inches high, of thin pale blue-green blown glass.

Right: Jug, Persian, 10th century AD. 5¾ inches high in pale green glass. *Photographs: Pilkington Museum*

Moulded jug in slagware. Late 19th century. Many of these jugs were made at the Sowerby glassworks, Newcastle upon Tyne, and carry the Victorian diamond registration mark. *Collection: Author*

and much of the new English lead glass was engraved in Holland. Much early wheel engraving is floral, and the most interesting is the Jacobite engraving. The most familiar pattern is a rose in full bloom, with an opening bud on one side, and a smaller bud on the other side. The large rose was supposed to represent the crown of England and the two buds stood for the Old Pretender and his son Bonnie Prince Charlie.

The brilliant English lead glass also was ideal for cutting – or, more accurately, grinding. This process was introduced from the continent in the reign of Queen Anne, and a great deal of 18th-century cut-glass is still available to collectors today, although the best is costly. Most of the vast quantity of cut-glass jugs, bowls and other wares produced in the prolific half century before

Wine jug in blue-green glass, 5¾ inches high, with swan neck strap handle. The body decorated with ribs and a spiral trail around the four lips. Spanish, mid-18th century.

1825 came from Irish factories. The largest were at Cork and Waterford and there were other glassworks at Dublin, Belfast, Newry and Londonderry. These factories were started by English craftsmen who left England when the Excise Act of 1777 imposed a hefty tax on English glass. The Act did not apply to Ireland, and when free trade was granted to Ireland in 1780 the temptation for English firms to start up there was almost overwhelming.

Nevertheless, the Irish competition did not kill the English

Jug, Wrockwardine, England, c. 1800 in green glass, decorated with mottling in white, green terracotta and pale blue glass. Height 7⅛ inches.
Photographs: Pilkington Museum

factories. The demand for cut-glass was so great that English factories were able to continue in production at the luxury end of the market. It is impossible in fact to tell whether most of this glass was made in England or Ireland. Some Waterford and Cork jugs were marked on the base, and some drawings of Waterford designs of the period still exist. But the famous blue tint, supposed to be peculiar to Waterford glass, is not a reliable guide, and it is safest to refer to cut-glass of this period as Anglo-Irish. Extremely heavy jugs would be more likely to be Irish, as the glass tax in England was levied by weight.

Left: Elegant Victorian glass claret jug.

Right: Jug 5½ inches high in green glass made at Nailsea. Into the surface of the four-sided body opaque white fragments of glass have been rolled.

The Irish glassworks went into decline after 1825, when Irish glass became liable for duty. Another factor in the decline of cut-glass was the American invention of pressed glass early in the 19th century. The Americans adapted the ancient method of making glass by pouring the metal into moulds for mass production, copying the designs of cut-glass. This type of glass was exported to Europe, and in 1833 W. Richardson bought American machines for making pressed glass and installed them in his factory at Stourbridge.

It seems likely that it was this imitation of cut-glass, which was so much cheaper but also vastly inferior to the real thing, that prompted Ruskin, that Victorian leader of taste, to be so derogatory. He declared, somewhat pompously: 'The peculiar qualities of glass are ductility when heated and transparency when cold ... all work in glass is bad which does not in a loud voice proclaim one or other of these qualities. Consequently all cut-glass is barbarous.'

Such dogmatic attacks, along with the heavy taxes, hastened the decline of cut-glass. At the same time it encouraged the development of new types of glass such as Nailsea. Because this was a type of bottle glass it was taxed at a lower rate than lead glass.

J. R. Lucas, a Bristol bottlemaker, established a glassworks at Nailsea in 1788, where he made jugs, mugs and flasks in a soft dark green glass, with flecks and loops of white to relieve the plain green. From 1810 Nailsea produced clear glass with stripes and loops in pink, blue or white. And from about 1830 onwards the loops were massed together, completely concealing the Nailsea glass. This type of glass was also produced at other factories such as Warrington, St. Helens, Newcastle, Sunderland, Stourbridge, Wrockwardine in Shropshire, and probably at Alloa in Scotland.

Some of the best 'Nailsea' was made at Warrington; yellow flecks in the dark glass suggest that it was made at Wrockwardine; and wherever it was made, 'Nailsea' glass, was often sold at country fairs and markets.

Simple jugs and mugs in bottle green, purple, Bristol blue or opaque white glass were also sold at country fairs towards the end of the 18th century. Some can still be found to carry gilded or enamelled inscriptions such as 'Be canny with the cream,' al-

though most such inscriptions easily wore off. But even without
their inscriptions these irregularly shaped jugs are charming.

The most famous coloured glass is of course Bristol blue – so-
called because the colouring constituent, called smalt and
imported from Saxony, arrived in Britain at the port of Bristol,
where glassmakers went from all over the country to buy it at
auction.

Another so-called 'Bristol' glass used for jugs and vases was
an opaque white colour, similar in appearance to porcelain.
This Bristol glass was usually decorated with hand-painted or
transfer-printed posies of flowers or of birds.

But some of the finest coloured glass was made in Europe.
When the Bohemian manufacturers found themselves unable to
compete with the magnificent Anglo-Irish cut-glass, they developed
a new type of clear, coloured glass in imitation of amethyst,
turquoise, rose quartz, jasper and other natural stones. They
also made vessels of cased glass in ruby red, blue and white,
with pierced decoration so that you could see through the top
layers of glass to other colours underneath.

When the Bohemian glass-makers showed this type of glass at
the Great Exhibition in 1851 it was a tremendous success, and
British manufacturers, notably at Birmingham and Stourbridge,
quickly imitated it. In fact it is now difficult to know whether a
piece of this cased glass was made in Bohemia or at Stourbridge.

Cased glass can have as many as four layers of coloured glass
in many different combinations, and sometimes is additionally
decorated with gilding and enamelling.

Another form of overlay that was much simpler and cheaper to
make is known as flashed glass. When the basic glass vessel was
cool it was dipped into molten coloured glass, and removed again,
so that it was covered with a thin film of colour. This film could
be cut through to reveal a pattern in the clear glass.

Some of the best British Victorian glass is clear-coloured
completely through the metal. Two types popular with collectors
today, and still reasonably priced, are cranberry glass and vaseline
glass. Cranberry is a light pinkish colour, and vaseline has a
yellowish tint. Other colours are different shades of greens,
amber, ruby and a deep purple which seems to be black until

held up to the light.

Many clear-coloured glass jugs are decorated in the Mary Gregory style. Mary Gregory was an artist at the Boston and Sandwich Glassworks in Massachusetts who became famous for her paintings of children at play in white enamel on coloured glass.

But although all glass of this type is known as Mary Gregory glass, she was not the originator of the decoration, merely copying with great success the work on glass imported from Bohemia. Most of the 'Mary Gregory' glass from Bohemia was made at the Hahn factory. The figures are always in white. Later Mary Gregory figures, on clear uncoloured glass, usually have flesh-coloured tints for the children's faces.

Another late-Victorian glass now sought after by collectors, but still reasonably priced, is slagware, which was perhaps inspired by the earlier Nailsea glass. Slagware is also known as 'end of the day' glass, or as vitro-porcelain, the name registered for it by Sowerby's glassworks at Newcastle upon Tyne. It was made by mixing silicates bought from steelworks in the form of slag drawn off molten steel at the end of the day. This was mixed with clear glass, giving a streaky, marbled effect. Sowerby examples often carry a peacock's head mark, and many examples from Sowerby and other glassworks bear the Victorian diamond register mark, from which the design can easily be dated.

Left: Heavy Georgian cut glass water jug. *Collection: Author*

Right: Fine late Victorian etched glass wine jug, bearing owner's initials. *Collection: Adrian Bowyer*

Chapter Ten
SILVER

Jugs and ewers were made from silver throughout Europe in the Middle Ages, lavishly ornamented, and often more than two feet high. But collecting silver of even comparatively recent date is a very expensive hobby, and magnificent early pieces are beyond the reach of all except museums and millionaire collectors.

The period of interest for most people, the great period of English silver, follows the Revocation of the Edict of Nantes in 1685, which forced Huguenot craftsmen to flee from France and start anew under more tolerant regimes. Naturally the refugees were not welcomed by the London silversmiths, who petitioned the King and the Goldsmiths' Company in protest against the new competition. But their complaints were of little use. Before long the Huguenot master craftsmen dominated the trade.

Probably the most easily collected silver jugs produced since this period are beer jugs and cream jugs, which were introduced when the practice of taking milk and sugar in tea began in the reign of Queen Anne. It was at this time that the first tea sets – teapot, cream jug and sugar bowl – were made.

There had been no call in the past for such small jugs, and the first cream jugs to be made for the tea table were miniatures of the larger jugs for beer and wine, usually of a circular baluster shape on a moulded foot, with a scroll handle. They were made with and without covers, and if there was a cover it would usually be domed, sometimes extending over the lip. Like the baluster beer jugs, the style was unpretentious, unlike the elaborate ewers still being made for the dining tables of the very wealthy. Some of the beer jugs had a double scroll handle, with domed covers, and scrolled thumbpieces.

The beer jug style was not, however, really appropriate for small cream jugs, and the silversmiths soon developed new shapes

94

that were more suitable. Many jugs were egg-shaped and set on three feet, with a domed cover. Pear-shaped jugs were also made, sometimes decorated with light engraving. They were normally on a round base soldered to the body of the jug, although on the better quality jugs there might be a fantail base of irregular shape. Some pear-shaped jugs have a handle set at right angles to the spout, and others made towards the end of the century have three cast hoof-shaped feet, a broad curved spout and a scrolled wire handle.

Chased rustic scenes were popular decoration for these jugs, and sometimes the handles were shaped like dogs. Vast quantities were produced, with many different variations on the basic shape. Samuel Meriton made many jugs with handles in the shape of entwined snakes.

The classic helmet shape, a well-established Huguenot design,

A pair of silver beer jugs bearing an inscribed coat of arms, made by Charles Wright, 1768. *Photograph: Sothebys*

always remained popular, but towards the end of the 18th century the quality of silver cream jugs deteriorated, and many of the inverted pear-shape and helmet shape jugs were made from parts stamped out in factories.

The practice of copying the shapes of larger jugs for small milk and cream jugs was eventually abandoned, chiefly because the narrow bases resulted in the small jugs being frequently knocked over, causing constant exasperation over spilt milk, no doubt, spoiling many a guest's fine visiting clothes. A lower and broader type of cream jug was introduced in the 1790s. Like the teapots of the period it was oval, with plain and slightly curved sides, a loop handle and narrow lip.

Gradually silver had come under the influence of rococo

20th-century elegance can often match the best from the past. This silver and glass claret jug was made by Omar Ramsden in 1929. *Photograph: Sothebys*

Right: A classic Georgian shape. This George III cream jug, by P. & A. Bateman, is dated 1791. *Photograph: Phillips*

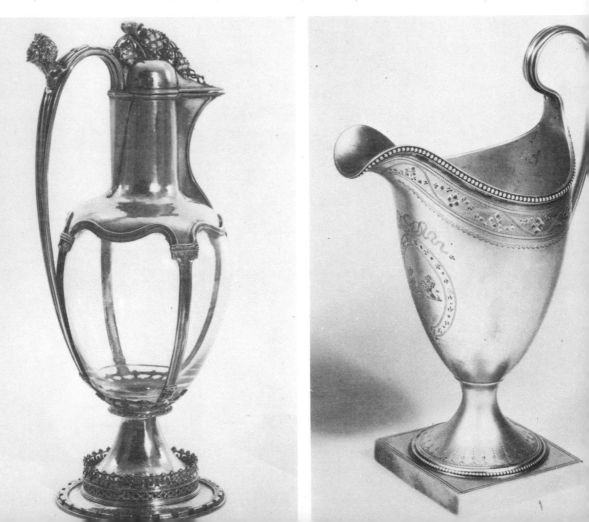

design. In the rococo period, for 30 years or so, everything was fancifully designed, with roughened surfaces, shells and scrolls, of naturalistic foliage. Jugs were made of much thinner-gauge silver than previously, and embossing was not only decorative, but also able to give strength to the metal. By the end of the period jugs were usually a mass of chased flowers and foliage, sometimes with embossed rustic scenes. Philippe Garden produced some very ornate beer jugs decorated with barley, hops and barrels. A pair of his beer jugs sold for £17,000 in 1969.

In the early 19th century the shape of cream jugs continued to follow the line of teapots, rather than the tall, slender jugs of the Adam period. By this time hot water jugs were being made as part of the tea set, and these also resemble the teapot but are taller. If there is any pedestal it is usually of three paw feet. Sometimes these hot water jugs are provided with a three-legged stand and burners shaped like ancient roman lamps. Unfortunately

Ornate decoration was a feature of Victorian silver jugs. These four are dated, left to right, 1861, 1880, 1855 and 1864. *Photograph: Phillips*

97

Stylish lines typify the Georgian period. This vase-shaped ewer with reeded bands and moulded feet is hall-marked 1792. It has escaped the attention of Victorian 'improvers' who would have loved to add profuse decoration. *Photograph: Phillips*

A fine Adam-style coffee jug by W. Holmes and N. Dumee, 1773. *Photograph: Sothebys*

many simple Georgian jugs were violated by Victorian engravers, who added over-elaborate and anachronistic decoration.

In the second half of the 18th century a curious cream jug in the shape of a cow, the cow creamer, was produced for the first time in England. These had been made in pottery previously in Holland, and while no one is certain who made the first silver cow creamer, it was a Dutch immigrant, John Schuppe, who made the vast majority of English cow creamers that come up for sale today.

The cow creamer is usually about seven inches long and three-and-a-half inches high. The curved tail serves as a handle, and the jug is filled through a hole on the back, the milk or cream being poured through the mouth. Some are in silver gilt and some are worked so as to imitate hide. Schuppe's creamers often have a fly surmounting the lid, to form a handle.

The Huguenots, who dominated English silver, also had influence in other countries, America for example. One Huguenot, Apollon Rivoire, migrated from Guernsey to America and set up in business as a silversmith in Boston. He changed his name to Paul Revere and trained his son Paul in the craft.

It was Paul Revere the Younger who became one of the leading rebels against the British, and his fame was recorded by Longfellow in his poem 'The Ride of Paul Revere'.

Revere became one of the most famous of American silversmiths, and his jugs, based on the Liverpool pottery jugs then being imported into America, are among his most admired works. The silver versions of Liverpool jugs have a bulging, barrel-shaped body. They are slightly flared at the foot and rim, have a triangular lip and a plain scroll handle.

Silver has always been expensive, and it was during the 18th century that a cheaper substitute, Sheffield Plate, was introduced. Basically Sheffield plate consists of a sheet of copper coated with an outer layer of an alloy of silver and copper. It was necessary

A four-piece Victorian tea-set with hot water jug, milk jug, teapot and sugar basin, embossed with cartouches, scrolls and foliage. Dated 1877. *Photograph: Phillips*

This profusely decorated tea and coffee set was made by Richard Sayer, Dublin, in 1835. *Photograph: Phillips*

for the outer coating to contain copper for the silver to adhere.

Among the most desirable Sheffield Plate jugs are the urn-shaped ones of the Adam period. As Sheffield Plate was designed to masquerade as silver, all the silver designs and shapes were imitated. Victorian Sheffield Plate carries ornate designs, but although the rococo of the previous century was copied, the jugs were not usually as tall as silver ones. The practical producers of Sheffield Plate had quickly learned the lesson that a reasonably low centre of gravity was of real value in a jug intended for household use.

In the 1840s and 1850s there was an exuberant flowering of naturalist decoration, in both silver and Sheffield Plate.

In Sheffield Plate jugs, handle sockets should be examined for damage and for earlier repairs, and there must always be a seam down the body on the handle side, which can be seen if you breathe gently on the plating. If you cannot see any seam it is likely that the jug has been reconditioned with new electroplating – anathema to the serious collector, who prizes the warm glow of the genuine piece, caused by the copper contained in the alloy.

Left: This fine silver quart-size jug with lid dates from the reign of George I.

Right: Magnificent Victorian beer jug, 17 inches high, 1865. *Photograph: Phillips*

The inside of a Sheffield Plate jug should be tinned. If it has a silvery appearance then once again it has probably been electro-plated.

The electroplate process itself was introduced in 1840 by Elkington's, who took out a patent. They were able to produce splendid looking jugs in all the silver shapes at much lower prices than either the silver or Sheffield Plate manufacturers.

Another cheap imitation of silver was a tin alloy known as Vickers White Ware, which was originated by John Vickers, a metal worker in Sheffield, in 1769. This could be polished to resemble silver, and many cream jugs were produced by Vickers.

One of the Sheffield Plate manufacturers, Thomas Low, made mounts for jasper ware jugs. He was one of the first Sheffield Plate manufacturers to mark his products.

101

Chapter Eleven
METAL

Jugs have been made of almost every common metal known to man – bronze, pewter, brass, copper. Bronze, for example, was used for splendid ewers in the Middle Ages; copper and pewter were much more commonly seen in household utensils. Copper was of special value in the kitchen. It has the advantage of being able to withstand higher temperatures than bronze, pewter and cast-iron, so that it is possible to stand a copper jug or pan on an open fire without ill-effects. In addition, for many people the soft red glow of copper makes it more attractive than any of the others.

In the 12th century brass and copper jugs were made at Dinant, along with other household articles which came to be known as Dinanteries. There was a thriving export trade. In the 15th and 16th centuries one of the chief centres for copper was Nuremberg in Germany, and the use of copper utensils was at its peak in Northern Europe in the 17th and 18th centuries.

Jugs were available in extremely wide variety. One of the most common was a jug with a broad body like a flattened sphere, a handle and spout, and sometimes short legs. These were used as water jugs and tea kettles, their broad flat bottom being an advantage in transmitting the heat from the fire to the water.

Wooden jugs were made with staves, in the same manner as barrels, and were often bound with copper strips. Large water jugs were also made in copper in the same shape as the staved wooden jugs. In Northern Germany a favourite shape was something like an upside-down ice cream cone, with a broad flat foot tapering to the top. In Southern Germany S-shaped and pear-shaped copper jugs were popular. In other areas a beak-shaped jug was common, rather like some earlier bronze jugs. One type of jug, known as the Rohrken, was an adaptation of the beaker, with the addition of a round pedestal, a spout, lid and handle.

This small, heavy brass jug was probably made in the 15th century. It bears a flourishing initial *M*, hammered in by some early owner to establish his claim to possession. *Collection: Adrian Bowyer*

There were in fact many variations in shape, some being like a double cone and others barrel- or egg-shaped. Some jugs would have a bulge in the middle of the body, in others the bulge would be at the bottom or at the top.

From very early times copper was produced in great quantity in the Balkans, and copper utensils have remained popular there up to the present day.

Balkan jugs are embellished with fine engraved or chased designs, or with punched decoration. Geometrical patterns predominate, with human or animal figures rarely seen. The most typical shape from the Balkans is a jug with a strikingly curved body. There is a tall narrow neck, a domed lid, a handle and a long spout branching out from the bulging lower body and curving boldly up to finish level with the lid. Another type has a much wider neck.

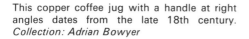

This copper coffee jug with a handle at right angles dates from the late 18th century. *Collection: Adrian Bowyer*

Today's mass-produced articles from the Balkans still follow the traditional designs.

In Britain pewter was more often used than copper for household utensils, although copper did become more popular in the 18th century. The British excelled in making pewter, and British pewter was admired on the Continent for its high quality. There are still English pewter jugs in existence from the late 16th century. They have shapes similar to silver jugs made at the same period.

Production of large ewers, sometimes known as hawksbill or ravensbill ewers, from the shape of their spouts, increased in the 17th century after the Church had sanctioned the use of pewter vessels for Communion.

In the home, pewter flagons were kept on British sideboards from 1700 onwards, to replenish diners' cups with wine or beer. The beer jugs were similar to silver ones in shape, although it is more common for pewter jugs to have spouts set at right angles

Late 18th century pewter. These two small wine measures from Jersey have heart-shaped covers, twin acorn thumbpieces and the G.R. stamp. *Photograph: Phillips*

to the handle. But the most common type of pewter jug is the flagon, which was used throughout Europe for serving wine or beer from the 16th century onwards. Early flagons are like a tall tapering cylinder on a wide base with a simple curved handle with a lid, and often a chairback thumbpiece to hold the lid back as the drink was poured out. By the middle of the 17th century the base of flagons was wider and they usually had a low belly, to give stability.

Irish and Scottish flagons were similar to the English in style, although many Scottish examples have inverted saucer-shaped lids and bands of moulded decoration, while some Irish ones have large curved handles.

Pewter measures were ubiquitous in taverns and hotels, and were in fact jugs from which a specified quantity of liquid refreshment could be poured. Some of the best wine measures were made in Scotland – the tappit hen, for example.

The largest size of the tappit hen contains exactly one pint – Scottish version. Perhaps Scottish drinkers had larger thirsts than their English counterparts, for the Scottish pint was equal to three English pints in the days before the measures of the two countries were standardised.

Left: The hollow, rounded handle and the folded seam at the base of this copper jug suggests a date of around 1840. *Collection: Adrian Bowyer*

Right: A rare 19th century pewter tavern jug. It is 10¾ inches high and holds one gallon. *Photograph: Phillips*

Left: Not surprisingly, few leather jugs of the 15th and 16th centuries have survived. This quite well-preserved jug bears an intriguing monogram at the base of the handle. It holds about a quart.

Below: The same quart leather jug with a smaller pint-sized model. Collection: Wally Clegg

European styles were more ornate, and were usually engraved. The Swiss jug known as the bell flagon was bell-shaped with a short high spout and a flat lid that could be unscrewed.

The most famous of Dutch pewter jugs is the Jan Steen. Like other Dutch pewter jugs it was pot-bellied, and has acquired its name because the Dutch painter Jan Steen portrayed it so often in his still-life paintings.

In the 19th century the pewter industry declined, largely due to the greater availability of new cheap alloys, and the massive increase in the production of pottery. Copper and brass jugs were made of thinner-gauge metal and were inferior in quality to earlier jugs.

Copper was also used in the 19th century to bind some of the attractive wooden wine jugs made in Brittany and Normandy.

Chapter Twelve
THE AMERICAN CONNECTION

∞

T he early settlers in America found it necessary to import
many domestic and luxury items from Europe. Among these
exports were vast quantities of jugs from Liverpool, Bristol and
Sunderland, many of them made especially for the new growing
American market.

Today many American collections and museums contain
examples of jugs made by Wedgwood, Josiah Spode, John Turner
and many other British potters, bearing transfer-printed decorations that are never seen in England. These jugs lauded American
heroes and famous victories, even when these were won at the
expense of the British!

One ship frequently shown on such jugs is the frigate *Con-
stitution*. Among the celebrated naval heroes depicted are Com-
modore Stephen Decatur and Captain James Lawrence: Decatur
was commander of the frigate *The United States* and captured
the British ship *Macedonian*; Lawrence commanded the
Chesapeake in her deadly battle with the British cruiser *Shannon*.

Of course, the faces of famous statesmen such as George
Washington and Benjamin Franklin helped to sell English jugs
to the American settlers too. And there is a series of transfer-
printed decorations commemorating the visit of the French
general Lafayette to America in 1824. This landmark of international recognition sometimes appears along with an engraving
of the surrender of General Cornwallis in 1781, which ended the
War of Independence.

The engravings used for these jugs were sometimes copied
from original drawings sent from America, or copied from prints
in books published there. Many of the engravings were executed
by the firm Bentley, Ware and Bourne of Shelton.

Glassware, silver and pewter were also sent to America. And

The peculiar relief design on this jug is meant to represent lines of cable. It commemorates the laying of the Atlantic cable. *Collection: Lesley Robinson*

just as England had imported Rhenish stoneware jugs in medieval times and copied the style and methods of manufacture, the Americans inevitably started to produce their own goods.

Indeed, even before the War of Independence there were flourishing glassworks in New Jersey and at Mannheim in Pennsylvania. The Mannheim enterprise was founded by a

German immigrant, Henry William Stiegel, who arrived in America in 1750 and married the daughter of an iron manufacturer.

He was a colourful, forceful character, who loved a luxurious life-style and was known to his workers, many of them skilled craftsmen from Europe, as The Baron. The glassworks he founded in 1756 produced coarsely painted bottles and jugs similar to those produced by small peasant manufacturers in Europe. But there was also much high-quality glass, wheel-engraved by German craftsmen. Stiegel produced a fine quality glass made in blue, green and amethyst shades, for instance, with mould-blown patterns incorporating a diamond daisy design.

The Baron's work set the standard for much that was to follow in America. Unfortunately he tried to expand his business too rapidly and became bankrupt. He found himself in jail for debt in 1774.

Another notable figure in the story of American glass was the Dutchman Caspar Wistar, who founded the Wistarburg Glassworks at Salem, New Jersey, in 1739. He also employed glassblowers from Europe and produced coloured glass.

Various other small glasshouses also started up in the southern part of New Jersey, producing jugs and other table ware. The characteristic decoration is known as lily-pad. The lily-pad is shaped from an applied layer of glass into one of three main shapes on the body of the jug: a slender stem with a bead-like pad; a wide stem with a small flattened pad; and a long, curving stem with an ovoid pad.

Eight glass-blowers from Pittsburgh moved to New York and founded the Lancaster Glassworks there in 1849. They produced jugs and bowls with lily-pad decoration in the South Jersey style until the factory closed at the end of the century.

As mentioned earlier American glass-makers played a prominent part in ending the dominance of English and Irish cut-glass. The most significant factor was, of course, the development of pressed glass by Deming Jarves, the son of a Huguenot immigrant. He introduced mechanical methods for moulding and pressing glass at the New England Glass Company at Cambridge, Massachusetts, about 1820, and in 1825 he started the Boston and Sandwich glassworks, where he employed skilled workers from

England, Ireland and Belgium.

Pressed glass, although much cheaper, never approached the quality of lead glass, however, so a market for good quality cut-glass did continue. William Leighton took advantage of this when he developed lime glass in 1864 at the Wheeling Glass Factory, West Virginia. It was cheaper, lighter, and faster cooling than the traditional lead glass.

Although most of the pottery used by the early settlers was imported, there were a few individual potters who made lead-glazed earthenware for local use from the second half of the 17th century. Some of the earliest stoneware was made by the Duche family in Philadelphia from 1692. Andrew Duche, one of the four sons of Antoine, founder of the firm, moved to Savannah where he discovered a fine china clay which was given the name *unaker*. He is believed to have been the first man to have made porcelain in America, using this clay. He shipped supplies of the clay to England, where it was used by the Bow porcelain factory.

The first really successful pottery factories in America were, however, those of J. Norton and C. W. Fenton at Bennington, Vermont.

Captain John Norton's factory made stoneware until it closed in 1894; while Christopher Fenton started his Bennington factory in 1847, producing white earthenware for domestic use. He also made jugs and vases in flint enamel ware, with applied relief decoration. These jugs have brilliant green, orange-yellow, and blue streaks fusing with a dark brown Rockingham glaze. Fenton also made American Toby jugs with a Rockingham glaze; and in the 1850s he made other jugs similar in style to those being made in the English Staffordshire potteries. He also produced scroddled ware, the American version of agate ware, with brown and green clays. Most of his jugs are unmarked. From 1853 until the factory closed in 1858 it traded under the name United States Pottery.

Although Andrew Duche may have been the first American to make porcelain, William Ellis Tucker was the first to produce it in commercial quantities. In partnership with Thomas Hulme he established a factory at Philadelphia in 1826 to make hard-paste porcelain. His early work was decorated in sepia, but after two years he began to produce pieces with enamel colours and gilding

The landing of Christopher Columbus in America was a popular subject for British potteries making jugs for export to America. The mark underneath this fine Copeland jug with white relief on a bright blue background shows that it was made specifically for sale in America. *Collection: Mrs. S. Davies*

in the style of Sèvres, showing American views, portraits or flowers.

The English influence was strong in the work of Edwin and James Bennett. James emigrated from England in 1834 and started a pottery at East Liverpool, Ohio. His brother Edwin moved to join him in 1841, and started his own pottery at Baltimore, Maryland, five years later. A great deal of relief-decorated Rockingham ware was made at the Baltimore factory. So were some very interesting jugs in a hard green or blue stoneware: these were often moulded, with hand-shaped handles, for example, or with fish in relief for decoration.

Apart from pottery, some interesting American jugs of the 19th century were made in tolerware. Tole, a French word meaning painted tin, was made in France from the 1740s, and mass produced from 1786. The term came to be applied to all objects of painted tin made at places such as Birmingham in the 18th and 19th centuries. American tolerware, also known as Pennsylvania tin ware, is japanned metal made chiefly in New York and New England from sheets of tinplate imported from England.

Chapter Thirteen
STRANGE SHAPES

Strange shapes seem to have fascinated ordinary people from earliest times, and jugs are extraordinarily well-suited to the potter's flights of fancy.

Stoneware jugs shaped like bears were made at Nottingham. Earthenware owl or Eulenkrug jugs first appeared at Nuremberg in the 16th century, painted in underglaze blue with feathers in applied relief. Some have armorial shields painted on their breasts: they were often given as prizes at shooting contests, and these arms may be the insignia of the prize-givers. In England owl jugs were made in slipware in the 17th century, and a few were made in salt-glaze stoneware in the 18th century.

But the strangest jug of all is that very English joker's jug, the puzzle jug, which defies anyone to drink from it without spilling the ale over his face and clothes. It was extremely popular in taverns, and the locals, having mastered the technique of drinking from their own puzzle jug, would roar with laughter as the stranger struggled to cope with its secrets.

The puzzle jug was made in varying designs in earthenware, delftware and stoneware. There is usually a hollow tube round the lip, opening into three or more spouts, and linked with the inside of the jug through the hollow handle. Sometimes there is a hole under the top of the handle. Before you can drink from a puzzle jug successfully you must close all the holes except one, and suck the liquid through that one hole.

The jugs usually carry a challenging rhyme, such as:

> Within this jug there is good liquor –
> Tis fit for parson or for vicar.
> But how to drink and not to spill
> Will try the utmost of your skill.

Another rhyme, seen on a Leeds puzzle jug is:

> Come, gentlemen, and try your skill –
> I'll hold you sixpence, if you will,
> That you don't drink this liquor all
> Unless you spill or let some fall.

These puzzle jugs remained popular throughout the 18th and 19th centuries, and varied in height between five and ten inches.

Another drinking vessel beloved by British topers was the posset pot. This had loop handles and spouts, and was usually

Father Neptune jug with sea-horse handle, hand painted. Made by Shorter and Son, England, about 1920. *Collection: F. Penny*

covered with a dome-shaped lid, sometimes with an ornamental knob. It was made in delftware in the 17th and 18th centuries and was used for the very popular, warming suppertime beverage traditionally drunk on Christmas Eve in Staffordshire and Derbyshire. Posset was made from hot ale, milk, sugar, spices, and was taken with pieces of toast or oatcake.

When it comes to fanciful and impractical shapes, the cow creamer must be in the first rank. Nevertheless it has always remained immensely popular, as an ornament, if not as a serviceable milk jug. Most pottery survivors available for collectors are either from Staffordshire or Swansea; the beginner, however, should be warned that many clever reproductions have been made in this century, and if he does not feel competent to judge

a cow creamer's genuineness himself he should buy only from a genuine dealer who will give him a proper receipt and guarantee.

The Staffordshire creamers often have brown and black markings, and some are in lustre. The typical Staffordshire cow creamer would have its tail curving on to the back, be mounted

Above: Two Satyr face jugs, one with bright polychrome colouring, the other in brown salt-glaze stoneware. *Collection: Adrian Bowyer*

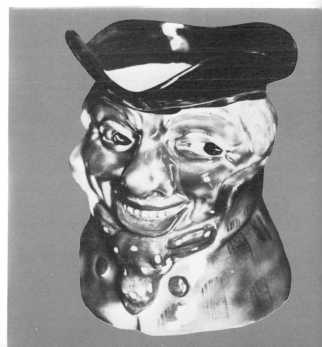

Right: Face jugs like this were produced in great quantities and variety at many English potteries during the 1930s. *Collection: G. Oakley*

on an oval green base with a large moulded daisy, and have a milkmaid beside the cow. Early specimens, however, had a flat rectangular base. Swansea cow creamers were often transfer-printed, and were on a rectangular base, with the tail curving to the flank of the cow rather than to its back.

Another peculiar jug you will certainly have seen in junk and secondhand shops is called snakeware, after the snakes and lizards that appear to crawl all over the surface. Most of these jugs were made in this century in Portugal, but their inspiration goes back to one of the greatest potters in history, Bernard Palissy, a French Huguenot who scorned to flee from persecution in his own country or to conceal his religious beliefs. The brilliant and realistic relief work on his pottery and the polychrome enamel glazing on his lead-glazed earthenware – green, blue, purple, yellow, dull red – did, however, attract the admiration of the royal family and gain him protection for many years. He was languishing in Bordeaux prison when Queen Charlotte ordered his release and appointed him 'workman in earth to His Majesty'. 'His heresy will not affect the colour of his glass or his pottery ware,' commented the Queen. Palissy was spared to work for many years, but he always remained outspoken, even after the Massacre

Left: Staffordshire face jug with bright polychrome colouring and a frog inside to startle the unwary. Early 19th century. *Collection: Wally Clegg*

Right: Staffordshire jug with Satyr head. Late 19th century. *Collection: Adrian Bowyer*

Face jug — Mephistopheles? — carrying basket of dead game. Underglaze colours, late 19th century. *Collection: F. Penny*

of St Bartholomew, and he was imprisoned again. Even a personal visit from the King failed to persuade him to renounce his beliefs and he died in the Bastille de Bucy in 1590. The jugs and other pottery made by Palissy and his followers in the 16th century must now all be in museums. But there are many fine jugs available still, done in the Palissy style, as many potters imitated his work, particularly in the 19th century.

The most successful of the imitators was another Frenchman, Arthur Corplet, who worked in Paris in the 19th century. The

Left: Cornucopia design for hand-painted 1920s style jug. Unmarked. *Collection: Brenda Jaquiss*

Right: Jug with camel spout in white delft. Probably 18th century. *Collection: Mrs. S Davies*

Minton factory in England also produced some Palissy-style jugs around the time of the Great Exhibition in 1851, which are fine examples of real craftsmanship.

The French porcelain factory of St Cloud, operating in the 18th century, produced some very unusual jugs in the form of birds and humans, and others with dragon-shaped handles.

The variety of different handles alone to be seen on old jugs is in fact astonishing. A collector who does not want to confine himself to collecting jugs of a specific factory or period, could build a fascinating collection based on as many different-shaped handles as possible.

The greyhound handle is fairly usual in 19th-century pottery, as is the rustic crabstock handle, but there are handles in other animal and human shapes. I have seen jugs with goat handles, and I have in my own collection an unusual Toby jug with the handle in human form, with arms clasped, rather in the way

118

knights clasp the arms in the brasses over their church tombs. Perhaps the handle is meant to represent Toby Fillpot after death. Another very attractive early 20th-century milk jug in a friend's collection has a brilliant white glaze, and the handle is in the finely modelled form of a cat, crouching as though it were trying to climb over the lip of the jug to get at the cream.

Left: This fine Minton Palissy-type jug has a pewter lid surmounted by a pottery jester's head. Late 19th century. *Collection: F. Penny*

Right: Belleek three-handled jug with hand-painted carousing marks.

The Fair Hebe jug, modelled by Jean Voyez. These jugs are all dated and signed. *Photograph: Sothebys*

Chapter Fourteen
COMMEMORATIVES

I suppose that the great era of commemorative jugs began with the development of transfer printing. But not all jugs of this type rely on a printed message.

One of the most famous commemorative jugs of all is the Lord Rodney jug, which was first produced in Derby porcelain, and has the head of the naval hero forming its mask lip. It was copied by the Leeds pottery and by Thomas Whieldon in Staffordshire.

Some relief-moulded jugs were also made as commemorative items. Famous cricketers like Box, Lillywhite and Pilch appeared in relief on early Prattware jugs, and in my collection I have a Staffordshire relief-moulded jug of Scottish interest: a recognisable portrait of Robert Burns appears on one side, and Sir Walter Scott on the other. The rest of the relief decoration consists mostly of thistles.

Another very unusual relief-moulded commemorative jug, of special interest to musicians, was sold at Phillips in London in 1975 to a collector of musical instruments. This jug commemorated John Distin and his four sons, who in their day were as famous as the Beatles. John Distin is regarded as the father of the brass band movement. He was a veteran of Waterloo and played the keyed bugle solo for the Grenadier Guards at the military review in Paris after the battle. When he left the army he formed a quintet with his sons to tour Britain and Europe. The Distin jug is six-sided and was made in white parian about 1850. It has relief portraits of the five Distins, and the sixth panel shows open music books. The handle is sculpted with wind instruments.

Doulton's of Lambeth also used relief busts and decoration in their commemorative jugs, issued towards the end of the 19th century, although these often also used applied lettering. The jugs issued in 1884 to commemorate the death of General Gordon

Right: A fine example of Liverpool black transfer-printing on a creamware jug made about 1805, shortly after the Battle of Trafalgar. The jug is 16 inches high and bears portraits of Nelson, the Earl of St. Vincent and Lord Duncan. *Photograph: Merseyside County Museums*

Below: A very interesting Crimean War jug. One side shows wounded soldiers on the battlefield; the other a grieving and destitute family. The jug publicises a fund to help war widows and orphans. The elaborate mark contains the date the design was registered, and incorporates the official registration mark, which protected the maker against copyists. *Collection: Lesley Robinson*

in that year used lettering to list Gordon's most renowned achievements.

These relief-moulded commemorative jugs are well worth seeking out, and there must still be many unrecorded jugs still waiting to be discovered. The same probably applies to transfer-printed commemorative jugs, for these jugs not only recorded the feats of the famous, but also the names of very ordinary people, often on the occasion of a wedding, for example.

I have already mentioned in a previous chapter the Sunderland Bridge jugs and the many transfer-printed jugs commemorating American victories, made in Staffordshire and Liverpool for export across the Atlantic. British victories were also extolled on jugs for the home market, the most common subject being the

Battle of Trafalgar and Lord Nelson. A rather more unusual jug I have seen recorded the death of Daniel O'Connell, the Irish patriot and statesman.

Royalty, naturally, dominates the field of commemorative jugs, and even today the most popular commemorative items manufactured are for royal occasions. But the reigning monarch has not always approved. George IV, for example, was annoyed at some of the commemorative china supporting his wife Caroline. The King had refused to allow Caroline to attend the Coronation in 1821 after evidence was given to the House of Lords that she was an adulteress. However justified the King was, the public sympathised with the slighted Caroline – a sympathy that was encouraged by Whig MPs for political reasons. The warmth of public feeling for Caroline was also extended to her daughter Charlotte, the only child of the royal marriage, who died tragically in childbirth after marrying Leopold of Belgium.

Any commemorative pieces of the coronation of Queen Victoria are rare, but there are still many jugs to be found celebrating the Golden Jubilee and the Diamond Jubilee.

The 19th century was a period of great political change, and some of the great political campaigns were recorded on jugs – the

Reform Movement of 1832, for example, and Free Trade in 1840. There seems also to have been a political motivation behind the manufacture of jugs ridiculing Napoleon. One, for example, shows the ferocious Russian bear squeezing Napoleon to his chest, and another depicts the great French leader as a capering Corsican monkey. The truth was that Napoleon's egalitarian politics appealed to many of the class-ridden ordinary British people, and he remained a worrying bogeyman to the British Government as long as he remained alive, even when he was imprisoned on remote St Helena. Anything that might lessen his popularity was to be encouraged.

One of the most popular subjects for transfer-printed jugs was the coming of the railways. The first locomotive to be illustrated

Three late 19th-century Doulton jugs, commemorating the deaths of probably the three most renowned men of the period: Disraeli, Gladstone and General Gordon. *General Gordon: Author's collection. Gladstone and Disraeli: Maureen Dennis's collection*

20th century coronation gifts are already in the collectable class, like these two jugs of the 1937 and 1953 Coronations.

The music-makers. This splendid parian jug has relief figures representing John Distin, the father of brass bands, and his four sons. *Photograph: Phillips*

on pottery was Blenkinsop's engine, which hauled a load of coal from the Middleton Colliery to Leeds in 1812.

Later jugs show the William the Fourth, Novelty, The Rocket, Fury, Express, railway stations and the marvellous new viaducts that appeared all over Britain as the 'navigators' pressed forward with their iron way.

One jug has prints of the opening of the Liverpool to Manchester railway line in 1830. On one side of the jug the familiar features of the hook-nose Duke of Wellington are seen in the front seat of a carriage, with a band blaring away in the next carriage. Another interesting jug made by Mintons in 1847 shows a stage coach contrasted with one of the new-fangled railway engines.

Left: This stoneware face jug of Wellington dates from between 1810 and 1820. *Collection: Adrian Bowyer*

Right: The more brightly coloured Staffordshire face jug was probably made after his death. *Collection: Adrian Bowyer*

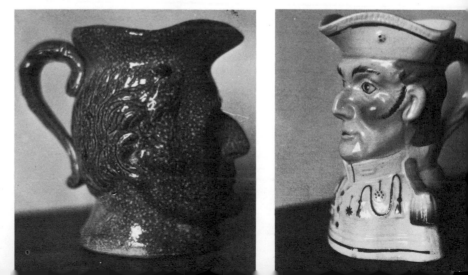

Chapter Fifteen
THE LARGE AND THE SMALL

The Victorian and Edwardian jug and basin sets, for the washstand, long despised, are now avidly collected. And rightly so. Not only do they provide examples of the whole history of English pottery in the 18th and 19th centuries, they are mostly elegant and pleasing decorative items in their own right. But the story of the jug and basin goes back much further even than Georgian times, although for most collectors the extravagant jugs made in the middle ages, and accorded the fancier name of ewers, must be out of reach because of their cost.

These ewers were not so much intended for the morning wash and brush up as for the use of diners at banquets. Because food in those days was always picked up with the fingers, etiquette decreed that a diner should wash his hands between courses. In the highest society circles the basins would be brought round to each person by pages after being filled with scented waters from the ornamental ewers. The page with the basin would be followed by another with a napkin for drying the hands. Common people presumably made do with licking their fingers.

The most elaborate and expensive ewers were made for church ceremonial. In the poem 'The Jackdaw of Rheims' the Cardinal is attended by boys 'in nice white stoles' carrying the rosewater for him to wash his hands, and it is when he removes his ring that the jackdaw pops down and steals it.

These ecclesiastical ewers were splendid objects made of the most valuable materials – gold, silver, silver gilt, ivory, bronze. The earliest examples from the 12th century were often made in the shape of animals – lions, dogs, dragons – and are known as aquamaniles. The water was poured through the mouth of the animal and the opening for filling was on the back. The handle was usually curved across the back, either in the form of the

animal's tail, or in the shape of a dragon or snake. Elaborate ewers of this type were also used in the richest homes, but less wealthy people made do with simpler ewers in copper, brass, pewter made in more conventional shapes. Animal-shaped ewers were made in England in the 13th and 14th centuries in lead-glazed earthenware, although pewter was the most common material used.

With the rise of the Staffordshire potteries in the 18th century, however, pottery vessels and dishes came into more widespread use, and jugs and basins to be placed on the wash stand in bedrooms were made in massive quantities. They continued to be produced well into the 20th century, until piped water supplies to every home became the norm.

Perhaps because it is only in comparatively recent years that the necessity for these jugs and basins disappeared they are a very late addition to the ranks of collectors' items. The Americans were quicker to realise their attraction than the British, and many thousands were exported across the Atlantic before British collectors began to take a real interest in them. Every British factory of note produced these jugs and basins, so theoretically it would be possible to build up a collection comprising examples of every different kind of pottery – if anyone has room for such a collection of large jugs.

It would be much more difficult to build up a collection of representative miniature jugs – but at least the space could be found even in a small flat. The most prolific maker of miniature china was William Henry Goss, who was chief artist and designer at the Spode factory in the 1850s and who eventually started business independently at the Falcon Pottery Works in Stoke on Trent. He copied ancient shapes in his ivory-coloured porcelain and added enamelled coats of arms to his miniature china, which was sold in the curio shops of every town in Britain – and also abroad, from South Africa to Jamaica. So vast was the production that it would make sense for a collector to specialise by merely collecting the miniature jugs he made.

Several of the 19th-century Staffordshire potters produced miniature tea sets, often transfer-printed, either as children's toys, or as advertising samples. There was also quite a vogue

Left: Art Deco ewer, typical of the 1920s. *Collection: Jean Crawford*

Right: Helmet shaped ewer and basin. Blue and white, with hand-coloured flowers. Edwardian. *Collection: Author*

for making miniature Toby jugs, mostly unmarked. In this century the Royal Worcester factory has produced some well-modelled tiny jugs. It would also be possible to build up a small collection of miniature silver jugs.

Cream jug from miniature tea-set, flanked by teapot and sugar bowl. Transfer printing in green, Davenport. 19th century. *Collection: Author*

Most of the output of W. H. Goss in the late 19th and early 20th century was of miniature china, including jugs in many different shapes. This rare Goss Toby jug, four inches high, is larger than most Goss items. *Photograph: Phillips*

Chapter Sixteen
THE ARTIST POTTERS

~~~~~~

In 1846 Henry Doulton succeeded his father John as head of the Doulton pottery at Lambeth. At first production of brown stoneware continued much as it had before, but when Doulton became friendly with John Sparkes, head of the Lambeth School of Art, he began to think along more enterprising lines.

It was the beginning of the period of the artist potters of the late 19th century. It was also the beginning of the period when the Doulton name achieved its greatest fame. Pupils of the school were given freedom to express their own decorative ideas in the brown stoneware, and when their jugs and vases were exhibited in 1871 they proved a commercial success. Encouraged, Doulton employed some of the best artists from the school, and in the last quarter of the century and the first few years of the 20th century the pottery flourished as never before. The quality and sophistication of decoration improved, and a number of new bodies were produced at the factory.

Silicon ware, for example, is a smooth, hard, unglazed stoneware. Carrara ware, named after the Italian white marble, is a semi-glazed white stoneware. And impasto ware was decorated before firing with thick paint that caused the pattern to stand out in relief on the finished jug.

Doulton believed in encouraging the pride of his employees in their art, and each artist was allowed to sign his pieces with initials on the bottom of the pottery.

H.B.B. stands for Hannah Barlow, probably the most famous of all the Doulton artists. She joined Doultons in 1871 from the Lambeth School of Art and was their leading artist until she retired in 1906. After some years her right arm became paralysed, but she trained herself to use her left hand, and carried on working. She specialised in spirited animal sketches – dogs, sheep or

horses – scratched on the moist clay, rather in the traditional sgraffito style. Sometimes the scratched lines were filled in with colour. *A.B.B.* was Arthur Barlow who worked at the factory from 1872 until his death only six years later. He did some incised work like his sister Hannah, and also produced floral patterns using blues and browns. *F.E.B.* or *F.B.* was another Barlow, Florence, who specialised in animals and birds. Once again, her early work was incised, but later she used coloured slips to build up a design

Above: The happy faces of a lucky collector: No wonder he's smiling. He bought these Martinware face jugs at a time when they could still be picked up cheaply.

Left: Some people love them; some people hate them, but the grotesque jugs made by the Martin Brothers at the turn of the century bring big prices in the salerooms. Every piece is individual: this leering face is a little more jovial than some.

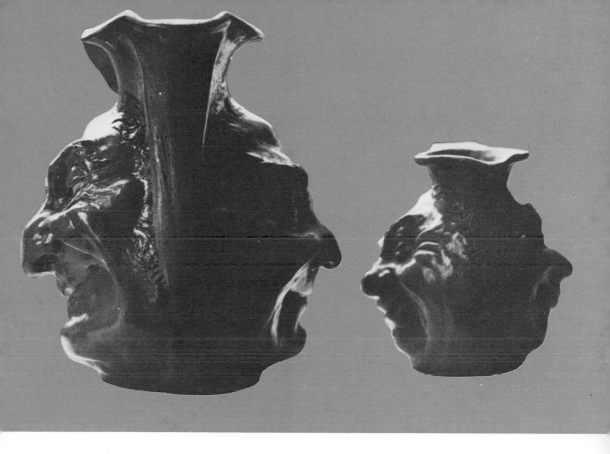

in relief on the main body of a jug or vase.

F.A.B. was Frank A. Butler, a deaf and dumb artist who produced work of high quality for more than 30 years from the 1870s onwards. *M.V.M.* was Mark V. Marshall, who designed and made some very large pieces. *E.S.* was Eliza Simmance, who used floral decorations and worked for Doultons into the 1920s.

Not all the bright pupils from the Lambeth School of Art went to work for Doulton, who became Sir Henry in 1878. One who got away was Walter Martin. He went to the Fulham Pottery, where John Dwight had worked and set up a workshop in King's Road, Fulham, in 1873, with his three younger brothers. They moved to Southall in 1877.

Much of their early work was blue and grey, and later examples used green and brown. They are best known for their grotesque

A front view of two Martinware face jugs. The work is extremely detailed.

131

birds and the face jugs with leering expressions. But much of their work is comparatively restrained, and always of high quality. Every piece was separate and individual, and most pieces were signed with the date and the name of the firm. Walter Martin was responsible for most of the throwing, glazing and firing, and Edward for most of the decoration. Charles was put in charge of the shop near High Holborn where they sold their ware. They continued in production until 1914.

The Martin Brothers were not the only potters producing slightly eccentric and unusual jugs. At Castle Hedingham in Essex the Bingham family worked in their ramshackle buildings from 1864 to 1905. A member of the Plymouth Brethren, Edward Bingham covered the walls of his home with religious texts. His family dug and refined the local clay. Their most elaborate pieces had moulded applied decoration, and sometimes were in white clay with blue, grey, green and brown glazes. Bingham also used coats of arms and classical motifs, and sold his ware from a showcase at the end of the garden, which carried the inscription: 'Original, Quaint and Classical'. But he was not a good businessmen, and the pottery ran into financial difficulties. The family eventually emigrated to America. Bingham's pottery carries a small relief of Hedingham Castle, and also the initials or signature of Edward Bingham.

Some curious jugs were also produced at the Rye Pottery in Sussex, established since the 15th century. About the middle of the 19th century the Mitchell family was in control of the pottery. Their hop jugs were decorated to a very high standard by William

Left: The signature and date on the base of a Martinware face jug.

Right: Another grotesque style of jug made by the Martin Brothers. The creature is completely imaginary.

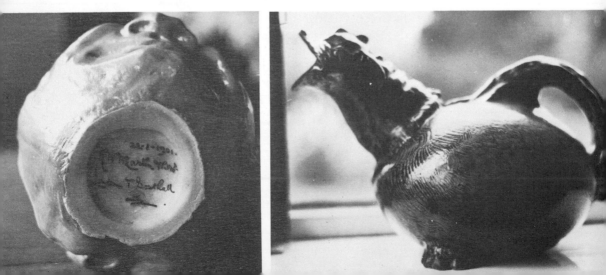

Mitchell, with three-dimensional hops and leaves covered with a good green glaze, which stand out against the dark brown streaked glaze of the body. The well-known Sussex pig jugs were also made at Rye in the 19th century, with a loose head used as a cup.

Down in Devon the Fishley family revived the local tradition of making sgraffito-decorated slipware harvest jugs at Fremington, near Bideford. Many interesting pieces were signed by

Left: The Martins did make conventional jugs. This tall stoneware one has a silver lid, almost a hark-back to the early German stoneware jugs imported into Britain.

Right: A miniature jug only 3 inches high, the delicate work on this jug is in complete contrast to the Martin face jugs. *Collection: D. Peyton*

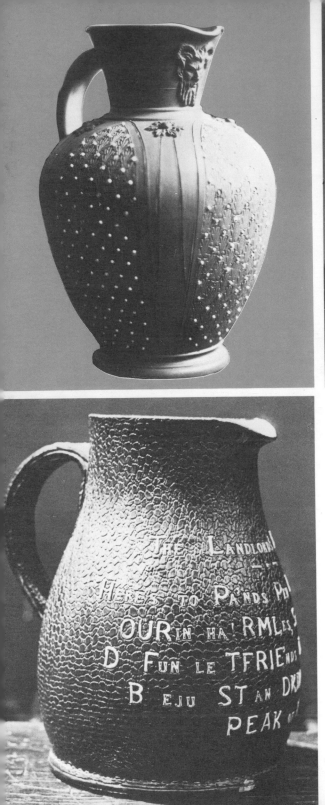

Above, left: This Doulton, Lambeth jug is dated 1876 and signed *HEH*. The glaze is typical Doulton. *Collection: F. Penny*

Above, right: An unglazed mask lip jug by Doulton, in silicon ware. About 1880. *Collection: F. Penny*

The potters at Doulton's Lambeth factory were always experimenting. One of the most curious kinds of jug they produced imitated leather very convincingly. The Landlord's Invitation on this one, when deciphered, reads
'Here stop and spend a social hour
In harmless mirth and fun
Let friendship reign
Be just and evil
Speak of none'
Collection: Mrs. S. Davies

Above: In Edwardian times, as fanciful Art Nouveau styles fell out of favour, design was in the doldrums. The small pre First-War cream jug on the left is pretty enough, but undistinguished. The 1920s brought the totally new Art Deco fashions and shapes. The jug on the right is typical early Art Deco, with a coloured rural cottage scene.

Below: The pure Art Deco styles tended towards the abstract. The practical side did not figure large in the designer's mind, and the handles on this jug and teacup made them difficult to hold. No doubt the eyes of the flappers were delighted. From a Shelley bone china tea set. *Collection: Author*

Edwin Beer Fishley, who died in 1912.

In Scotland too, there was an artistic flowering, at the Fife Pottery at Gallatown, near Kirkcaldy. Some extremely fine highly decorated hand-painted pottery was produced here between 1880 and 1930. Now well-known as Wemyss ware, after the nearby Wemyss Castle, the inspiration for the bold and unmistakable

Scotch and soda, sir?
The Scotch came from
Glasgow, the soda from
Dublin. These advertis-
ing face jugs were made
in France at Sarregua-
mines.

decoration was a young Czech called Karel Nekola who went to work for the Heron Family, and trained many fine Scottish decorators. Wemyss ware is bold and colourful. The most frequent patterns are floral and the big red cabbage rose almost came to be regarded as the Wemyss trade mark. Fruit and insect painting were also employed. Some subjects are rarer than others, particularly those showing animals and people. There are two very interesting jugs in the Perth Museum, one depicting Kate Glover, The Fair Maid of Perth, and the other a local town official, George Fell.

The quality of work declined after the death of Karel Nekola in 1915, and the moulds and rights of the firm were taken over in 1930 by the Bovey Tracey pottery in Devon. Joseph Nekola, Karel's son, moved to the new pottery and continued to produce Wemyss patterns there until he died in 1952.

Now that the famous annual Grosvenor House antiques fair has thrown open its doors to works of craftsmanship of the 1920s and 1930s, there is bound to be a new impetus to the collecting of bygones from the first half of this century. As Victorian jugs become scarcer this is a period that the new collector should study. Many interesting jugs of real quality were made in this period and eventually some will come to be recognised not only as attractive and worthy of collection, but valuable as well.

The claims of Wedgwood are already fully recognised, of course,

136

An attractive little jug, handed out by a Doncaster grocer to his best customers.

Below, right: A splendid and colourful Coronation jug commissioned by Dewar's whisky from the Royal Doulton Pottery. *Collection: F. Penny*

and exceptional items like the First World War Toby jugs made by the Royal Staffordshire pottery already bring good prices at the leading auction rooms.

I have already referred to the Royal Doulton Toby and character

jugs still in production, but inevitably collector's items of the future. But what of the many earlier Royal Doulton jugs, some of high quality but now out of production for many years? The early Royal Doulton jugs did in fact carry on the tradition of the late 19th-century Doulton jugs. The Royal Doulton potteries of today are in fact on the site of a factory acquired at Burslem in Staffordshire in 1882.

Among the early 20th-century jugs from Royal Doulton are the white salt-glaze stoneware face jugs of Dickens characters designed by L. Harradine and first produced just before the 1914 war. One curious type of jug was made to simulate leather, complete with seam marks and a strap-like handle. But there are many other Royal Doulton jugs of quality that can still be bought quite cheaply by a collector. Some of these were used for advertising whisky and other drinks: which suggests another area in which a collection could be formed at very reasonable prices.

Above: Two very fine face jugs from the Sarreguamines pottery. About 10 inches high. 19th century. *Collection: F. Penny*

Below: Two Auld Lang Syne jugs. A 19th-century stoneware one with black transfer printing, and a colourful Royal Doulton jug, typical of the many fine jugs made by this firm. *Collections: Lesley Robinson and Author*

BIBLIOGRAPHY

LIVERPOOL POTTERY by Alan Smith (Liverpool City Museums).

GOOD SIR TOBY by Desmond Ayles (Doulton & Co. Ltd., 1955).

SUNDERLAND WARE edited by J. T. Shaw (Sunderland Museum).

COLLINS ENCYCLOPAEDIA OF ANTIQUES (1973).

ENGLISH GLASS by W. A. Thorpe (A. and C. Black 1935).

SILVER by Gerald Taylor (Penguin Books 1956).

AMERICAN POTTERS AND POTTERY by John Ramsay (Hale, Cushman and Flint, 1939).

A COLLECTOR'S HISTORY OF ENGLISH POTTERY by Griselda Lewis (Studio Vista, 1969).

VICTORIAN POTTERY by Hugh Wakefield (Barrie & Jenkins, 1962).

INDEX

Advertising jugs, 136, 137, 138
Alloa, 91
Anglo-Irish glass, 90
Apostle jug, 31
Aquamaniles, 125
Art Deco, 135
Astbury, John, 22
Astbury, R. M., 28
Auld Lang Syne jugs, 139
Austin, Jesse, 65

Baltimore, Maryland, 111
Barlow, Arthur, 130
Barlow, Florence, 130
Barlow, Hannah, 129
Barnstaple pottery, 14, 15
Baxter, George, 65
Bear jugs, 19, 21
Belfast, 89
Bell, J. and M.P., 34
Bellarmine, 17, 18
Belleek, 119
Bennett, Edwin and James, 111
Bennington, Vermont, 110
Bentley, Ware and Bourne, 107
Bianca sopra bianca, 11
Bideford pottery, 14, 133
Bingham, Edward, 132
Black basalt, 50, 51, 53, 54, 57
Bloodsworth of Lambeth, 21
Boote, T. R., 34
Boston and Sandwich
   glassworks, 93
Bourne, William, 21
Bovey Tracey pottery, 136
Bow porcelain, 78
Brampton stoneware, 21

Brass, 103, 106
Bristol, 10, 67, 81, 82, 91
Bristol blue, 91, 92
Bronze, 102
Burns (Robert) jug, 26, 120
Butler, Frank, 131

Cabbage leaf jug, 78
Caesar (Julius) jug, 29
Cambridge, Mass., 109
Caneware, 55, 56
Carrara ware, 129
Cased glass, 92
Castleford jugs, 25
Castle Hedingham, 132
Caughley, 81
Cauliflower ware, 50
Cernuccus jug, 30
Champion, Richard, 82
Chelsea porcelain, 76–78, 81
Chesterfield stoneware, 21
Chesterton, G. K., 36
Churchill (Winston) toby jugs,
   37
Claret jugs, 90, 96
Cobalt blue, 11
Cologne ware, 18
Columbus jug, 111
Cookworthy, William, 81, 82
Copeland, 27, 34, 111
Copper, 102, 103, 105, 106
Copper lustre, 67, 69, 73
Cork and Edge, 34
Cork glassworks, 89, 90
Corplet, Arthur, 117
Cottage ware, 68
Cow creamers, 98, 99, 114–116

141

Cranberry glass, 52
Creamware, 58, 60, 61, 62
Cricket commemorative jugs,
  120

Davenport, 128
Delftware, 10, 11, 12, 14, 59
Denby pottery, 121
Derby, 80, 120
Devon potteries, 13, 14, 133,
  136
Dickens character jugs, 138
Distin (John) jug, 120, 124
Doulton and Watts, 21
Doultons of Lambeth, 120, 122,
  123, 129–131, 134; Royal
  Doulton, 37, 47, 137, 138
Dublin glassworks, 89
Duche family, 110
Dwight, John, 18, 19, 85, 131

East Liverpool, Ohio, 111
Electroplate, 101
Elers brothers, 19, 20, 22
Elwes, Henry, 39
Engraved glass, 87, 88
Ewers and basins, 125–127

Face jugs, 21, 115, 116, 117,
  138, 139
Fair Hebe jug, 24, 25, 27, 28
Fair Toxophilite, 15
Fairyland lustre, 58
Famille verte, 77
Farmer's Arms jug, 63
Father Neptune jug, 113
Fenton, C. W., 110
Fife pottery, 135
Fillpot, Toby, 27, 36, 39, 138
Fishley family, 14, 133, 134
Flashed glass, 92
Freemasons' jugs, 72, 73
Fremington, 133
Fulham pottery, 18, 19, 131

Garden, Phillipe, 97
General Gordon jug, 120
Goat and Bee jug, 76, 77, 78
Goss, W. H., 16, 127, 128
Gould, F. Carruthers, 43, 46, 47
Green, Guy, 59
Gregory (Mary) glass, 93
Greyhound handles, 118

Hancock, Robert, 84
Harlow, 13
Harradine, L., 138
Harvest jugs, 13, 34
Henley on Thames, 85
Herculaneum pottery, 61, 62,
  63, 65
Holland and Green, 34
Hulme, Thomas, 110
Hunting jugs, 21, 58

Irish glass, 89–91
Ironbridge, 81

Jackfield ware, 14
Jacobite glass, 88
Jan Steen jug, 106
Jarves, Deming, 109
Jasper dip, 54
Jasperware, 52, 54, 101
John Distin jug, 120, 124
Julius Caesar jug, 29

Lafayette, 107
Lambeth face jugs, 21
Lambeth pottery, 11
Lancaster glassworks, New
  York, 109
Lawrence, James, 107
Lead glaze, 11, 12
Leeds pottery, 34, 61, 120
Leighton, William, 110
Lily-pad decoration, 109
Liverpool, 10, 67, 81, 121
Londonderry glassworks, 89

Long Eliza, 81
Lord Rodney jug, 80, 120
Low, Thomas, 101
Lowestoft, 78
Lucas, J. R., 91
Ludwigsburg, 78
Lustre jugs, 66–75

Mackeig-Jones, Daisy, 58
Malling jugs, 10
Mannheim, 108
Marshall, Mark V., 131
Martin brothers, 130, 131, 132
Mary Gregory glass, 93
Masonic jugs, 72, 73
Mason's Ironstone China, 30,
    33, 34, 35
Meigh, Charles, 29, 31
Meissen porcelain, 76, 79
Meriton, Samuel, 95
Millfield pottery, 70, 75
Minster jug, 29
Minton, 34, 118, 119, 124
Mitchell, William, 132, 133
Mocha ware, 15, 16
Moonlight lustre, 51, 58
Morley, Francis, 34
Morleys of Mughouse Lane, 20
Murray, Keith, 58

Nailsea glass, 90, 91, 93
Napoleon jugs, 123
Nekola, Karel, 126
Nelson jugs, 14, 122
Neptune (Father) jug, 113
Newbottle pottery, 71
Newcastle Upon Tyne, 88, 91,
    93
New England Glass Company,
    109
New Hall, 79, 81, 82
New Jersey, 108, 109
Newry, 89
New York, 109
Norton, J., 110

Nottingham jugs, 20, 21

Palissy, Bernard, 116, 117, 118,
    119
Parian, 27, 34, 120, 124
Parnell, Paul, 38
Pearlware, 52
Pennsylvania, 108
Pennsylvania tinware, 111
Persian glass, 87
Pewter, 104, 105
Philadelphia, 110
Pittsburgh, 109
Plaster of Paris moulds, 22
Plymouth, 81
Posset pot, 114
Pratt, F. and R., 14, 65
Prattware, 13, 14, 15, 120, 122
Pressed glass, 91, 110
Punch jug, 49, 70
Punch and Judy toby jugs, 42,
    46
Puzzle jugs, 12, 21, 112–113, 118

Queensware, 50

Railway jugs, 123, 124
Ravenscroft, George, 84–87
Red stoneware, 19, 22, 55
Registration marks, 29, 31, 32,
    93
Resist lustre, 67, 73, 74
Revere, Paul, 62, 99
Rhenish stoneware, 17, 20
Richardson, W., 91
Ridgway, 31, 35
Robert Burns jug, 26, 120
Rockingham glaze, 39, 110
Rodney (Lord) jug, 80, 120
Rohrken, 102
Roman glass, 87
Rosso Antico, 55
Royal Doulton, 37, 47, 137, 138
Royal Staffordshire Pottery,
    43, 46

Royal Worcester, 40, 128
Ruskin, 91
Rye Pottery, 132

Sarruegamines, 139
St. Helens, 91
Sadler, John, 59, 60
Sadler and Green, 59, 60, 61,
   63, 64
Salem, New Jersey, 109
Salt glazing, 18, 19, 20, 22, 23
Satsuma, 81
Satyr jugs, 115, 116
Savannah, 110
Savoy glassworks, 85
Schuppe, John, 98, 99
Scott, Sir Walter, 120
Sgraffito, 11, 13, 14
Sheffield, 66
Sheffield plate, 66, 99–101
Shelley bone china, 135
'Shining black', 14
Silicon ware, 129, 134
Silver lustre, 66, 73, 74
Simmons, Eliza, 131
Slagware, 88, 93
Slipware, 12, 13, 112
Snakeware, 116
Sowerby glass, 88, 93
Spode, Josiah, 64, 65
Sprimont, Nicholas, 76, 77
Staffordshire dog jug, 114
Steen (Jan) jug, 106
Stephenson, Robert, 69
Stiegel, Henry William, 108
Stone china, 31
Stourbridge, 91, 92
Sunderland, 46, 66, 67, 69, 71,
   91
Sussex pigs, 133

Tam O'Shanter jugs, 24, 31, 33,
   44
Tappit hen, 105
Tigerware, 17, 20

Toby jugs, 23, 36–47, 118, 128,
   138
Toddy jugs, 21
Tolerware, 111
Toxophilite, Fair, 15
Transfer printing, 59–65, 121,
   128
Tucker, William Ellis, 110
Turner of Lane End, 25, 32
Tythe pig, 45, 46

United States Pottery, 110

Vaseline glass, 92
Venetian glass, 83, 85
Verzelini, 83
Vickers, John, 101
Vitro-porcelain, 93
Voyez, John, 24, 25, 27, 39, 40,
   41, 48

Wall, Dr., 80
Warrington glass, 91
Washington, George, 107
Waterford glass, 90
Wearmouth Bridge, 68–75
Wearside Pottery Co., 70, 75
Wedgwood, Josiah, 25, 39, 40,
   41, 48–58, 60, 61
Wedgwood, Sarah, 50–52
Wellington jugs, 124
Wemyss ware, 135–136
Wesley, John, 48
Wheeling glass factory, 110
Whieldon, Thomas, 14, 49, 120
Wilcock, John, 66
Winston Churchill toby jugs,
   37
Wistar, Caspar, 109
Wistarburg glassworks, 109
Wood, Ralph, 23, 27, 28, 41
Wooden jugs, 102–106
Wright, Charles, 95
Wrockwardine, 89, 91
Wrotham, 13
Worcester, 64, 65, 78, 80, 81, 82